Micro Macramé

Micro Macramé

25 Superfine Jewelry Projects

Jenny Townley

Micro Macramé
A QUARTO BOOK

First edition for North America
published in 2016 by
Barron's Educational Series, Inc.

All inquiries should be addressed to:
Barron's Educational Series, Inc.
250 Wireless Boulevard
Hauppauge, New York 11788
www.barronseduc.com

ISBN: 978-1-4380-0725-0

Library of Congress Control No.:
2015956700

QUAR.NEMA

Conceived, designed, and produced by
Quarto Publishing plc
The Old Brewery
6 Blundell Street
London
N7 9BH

Senior editor: Lily de Gatacre
Senior art editor: Emma Clayton
Copy editor: Caroline West
Designer: Tanya Devonshire-Jones
Photographers: Simon Pask,
                          Phil Wilkins
Proofreader: Julia Shone
Art director: Caroline Guest

Creative director: Moira Clinch
Publisher: Paul Carslake

Color separation in Hong Kong by
Bright Arts Ltd
Printed in China by 1010 Printing
Limited

9 8 7 6 5 4 3 2 1

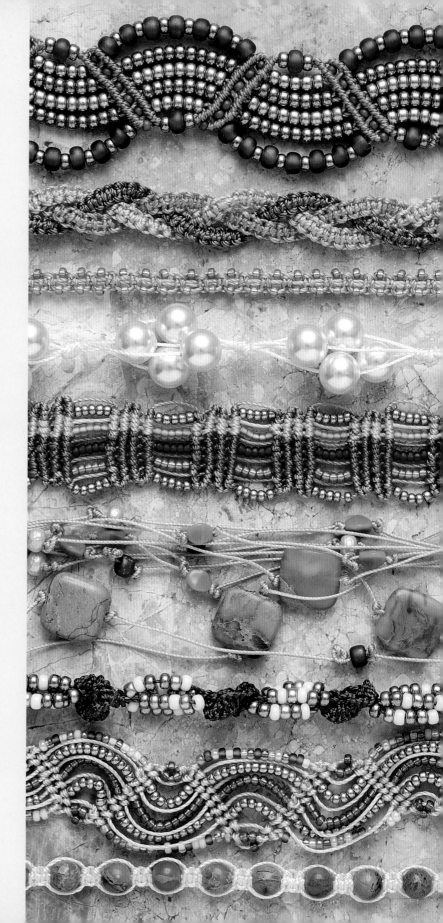

Contents

8

Knots, Tools, and Techniques

34

Beginner Projects

58

Intermediate Projects

86

Advanced Projects

Meet Jenny

Micro macramé is a wonderful hobby and is growing in popularity. My own inspiration came from looking at some of the intricate patterns and pieces that can be created in just about any color you like. Mixing textures and colors is fun, and many different looks can be created from just one simple pattern. In this book you will find a wealth of different pieces to create.

Micro macramé can be a time-consuming hobby, but once you have mastered the basic knots, there really is no end to what you can do—and you never really stop learning new techniques. Never be afraid to try: Practice does indeed make perfect in the end. I am self-taught in the art of micro macramé and it took me several attempts to master some of the trickier knots, so don't be put off by an early mistake. We all make them!

Just let your imagination loose and try mixing different color palettes. You will be pleasantly surprised. I have tried to select a wide variety of color palettes in this book to give you an idea of some of the different ways that you can mix colors.

Please feel free to pop over and visit my website and see some more of my micro-macramé designs, as well as examples of my other passion: sea glass jewelry.

When I'm not knotting, you can find me at the beach!

L. Townley

Jenny Townley
www.micromacrame.net

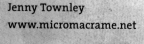

About This Book

The core of this book is the collection of 27 projects that guide you through the creation of some beautiful jewelry pieces. First, you will learn the basics of choosing your tools and materials, a few useful design tips and jewelry-making techniques, and how to tie the key micro-macramé knots.

The Knot Directory

Here, you'll be introduced to the core knots that will start you on your macramé journey and will feature in the projects later in the book.

Follow the photographs and instructions to build your knot step by step

Right and left versions of the same knot are explained separately to make things simpler

The knots are demonstrated with 2-mm Chinese knotting cord so the details are easy to see

The Projects

This collection of micro-macramé jewelry projects allows you to build and showcase your jewelry-making skills. Follow the project stages precisely or take inspiration and adapt, develop, and create your own personal designs.

A complete list of the tools and materials needed for this project

The knots you will need to know for this project are listed here

Beautiful styled photography showcases the finished pieces

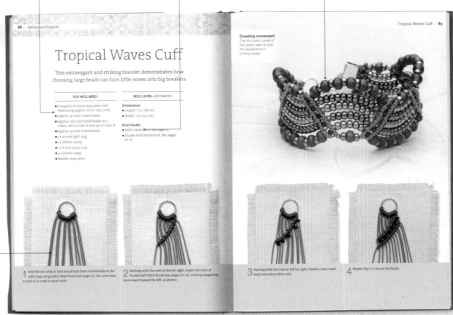

Clear step-by-step instructions guide you through each project

Projects are divided into beginner, intermediate, and advanced chapters to help you choose the right project for you

Large photographs of each stage help you to check your progress as you go

Some projects feature annotated photographs to point out the key techniques and knots

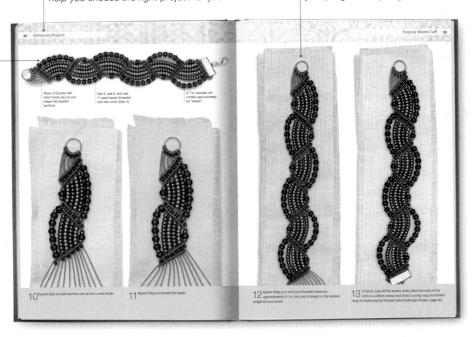

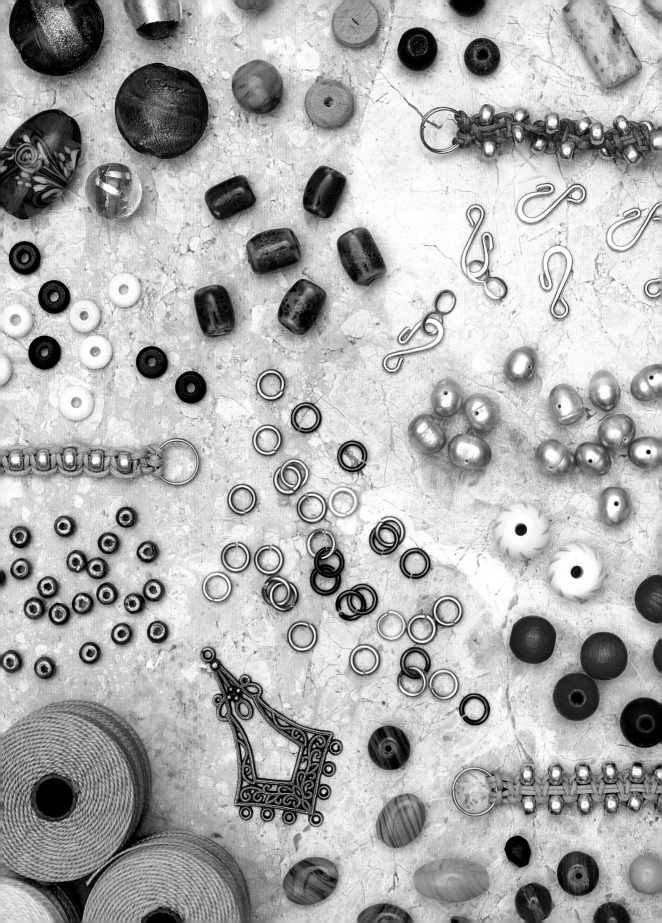

1

Knots, Tools, and Techniques

The wonderful thing about micro macramé is that you don't have to buy lots of expensive equipment and learn lots of complicated techniques before you can create something lovely. This section will introduce you to the key knots that will appear in the projects and give you some guidance to set you on your way.

Knot Directory

Before you embark on any of the micro-macramé jewelry projects in this book, take some time to get to know, understand, and practice the knots that you will be using.

Practice Makes Perfect

It's important to familiarize yourself with the most common macramé knots before you embark on a project, so take a little time to learn these basic skills first. All the projects in this book are created using just eight key knots, so mastering them will not take very long.

You will generally be using very fine micro-macramé cord to create the superfine and delicate project designs but, if you are a beginner, you might find it a little easier to learn the knots using slightly thicker cord. This will make it easier to see what you're doing, spot where you've got it right, and, maybe more importantly, where you've got it wrong. Also, the slightly thicker cord is a little bit easier to work with, and to unpick, so you can practice the

same knot over and over again without wasting lots of cord. In this section, the knots are demonstrated with 2-mm Chinese knotting cord.

Choosing Knots

If you are looking to create a pattern of your own, then you need to think about what type of knots you will use to make your masterpiece. If you are looking to produce a particularly intricate pattern, stick with a knot that you are comfortable with, as well as one you can tie at its tidiest, because an intricate pattern will show up the tiniest of imperfections and irregularities in tensions.

You also need to think about whether you want to include beads with your knots. The basic Square Knot (see page 12) is popular in many designs and is always

Lark's Head Knot

The Lark's Head Knot is a really useful little knot and is made in just a few quick, simple steps. It is most often used to attach cords to findings, and most projects in this book begin with a Lark's Head Knot.

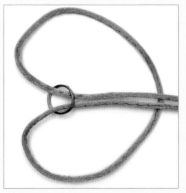

1 Fold the cord in half and then place the folded section through the split ring, as shown.

2 Pull the looped end forward, over the cord ends, then draw the two ends through the loop.

3 Pull the two ends to tighten the knot.

a safe bet to begin with. However, adding some beads will transform the piece of jewelry from something plain to one that is both elaborate and interesting. You can also create a variety of looks using different colors if you add some beads to your knots.

The Overhand Knot (see below) is often overlooked and is generally only used to tie a few cords together in one simple step. However, if it is made with several cords in a row, it can be made into a very lacy pattern. After all, most hammocks are made with overhand knots! On a much smaller scale, this could be used to create a very feminine cuff, with or without beads.

Knots can also look quite different, depending on the type of cords you choose. Try creating a line of Spiral Knots (see page 13) in hemp and one in a lightly waxed soft cotton cord, and you will see a huge

difference. Simple knots can take on a whole new look when combined with other knots in a pattern. Row after row of Double Half Hitch Knots (see pages 16–17) alone, for example, would look completely different if broken up with several rows of alternating Square Knots. Try combining different knots in a pattern to create your own unique look and design. Learn the basics and then let your imagination loose—you may be pleasantly surprised at what you can achieve.

Overhand Knot
A versatile and really simple knot that just slips into its position and ties onto itself.

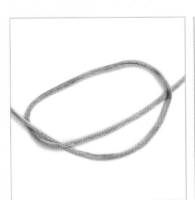

1 Make a loop with your cord with the left end over the right end. Pass the right-hand cord around and through the loop.

2 This can also be created by starting with a loop with the right cord over the left and then wrapping the left-hand cord over and through.

3 Pull the two ends to tighten the knot.

Square Knot

The Square Knot is the basis for the majority of simple micro-macramé patterns. It is most frequently used in friendship-style bracelets. The Square Knot is usually made with an even amount of cords. It is worked with the outside cords being placed over the two inner cords.

1 Start with four cords. To work this onto a split ring, fold two lengths of cord in half and attach each to a split ring using a Lark's Head Knot (see page 10) to give you four working cords.

2 Place the right-hand cord over the central "lazy" cords and under the outer left cord. Then take the outer left cord and place it under the two lazy cords and pull up through the loop.

3 Pull the ends of the outer cords to tighten.

4 Place the outer left cord over the two lazy cords and under the outer right cord. Then place the right cord under the two lazy cords and pull up through the loop.

5 Pull the ends to tighten and complete one Square Knot. Repeat Steps 2–4 until the knotting is the desired length.

Spiral Knot

This knot is also known as a Half Knot because it is basically half a Square Knot (see left). It creates a very pretty twisted spiral cord, so is perfect to use for making a necklace.

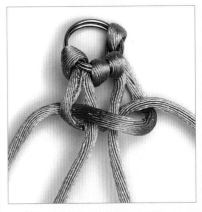

1 Start with four cords. To work this onto a split ring, fold two lengths of cord in half and attach each to a split ring using a Lark's Head Knot (see page 10) to give you four working cords.

2 A spiral knot is created by repeating Step 2 of the Square Knot over and over again. Place the right-hand cord over the two central "lazy" cords and under the outer left cord.

3 Take the outer left cord and pass it under the two lazy cords and pull up through the loop.

4 Pull the ends to tighten and complete one Spiral Knot.

5 Repeat Steps 2–4 until the knotting is the desired length. The tighter these knots are tied, the more attractive the spiral will be.

Left Full Loop Knot

This knot may appear more complicated but it is created with just a few steps and as the name suggests is worked from left to right. It is another knot frequently used in friendship-style bracelets.

1 Start with four cords. To work this onto a split ring, fold two lengths of cord in half and attach each to a split ring using a Lark's Head Knot (see page 10) to give you four working cords.

2 Place the outer left cord over the next cord to its right and pull up through the loop. Repeat once.

3 Pull the ends of the cords to tighten the knot.

4 Repeat Steps 2–3 using the same original outer left cord but by placing it over the next free cord.

5 Keep repeating Steps 2–3 until the outer left cord becomes the new outer right cord. Then begin again with the new left-hand cord. Keep knotting until you reach the required length.

Right Full Loop Knot
The same as the Left Full Loop Knot, but worked from right to left.

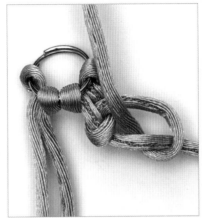

1 Start with four cords. To work this onto a split ring, fold two lengths of cord in half and attach each to a split ring using a Lark's Head Knot (see page 10) to give you four working cords.

2 Place the outer right cord over the next cord to its left and pull up through the loop. Repeat once.

3 Pull the ends of the cords to tighten the knot.

4 Repeat Steps 2–3 using the same original outer right cord but by placing it over the next free cord.

5 Keep repeating Steps 2–3 until the outer right cord becomes the new outer left cord. Then begin again with the new right-hand cord. Keep knotting until you reach the required length.

Double Half Hitch Knot

This is a trickier knot and one that requires attention to tension and detail. In fact, the Double Half Hitch Knot is said to be the most difficult knot to master. It is shown here with two cords attached to a split ring, giving you four cords to work with.

We will start by explaining the Double Half Hitch Knot working from left to right, and using the outside left cord as a "filler" cord.

DOUBLE HALF HITCH KNOT LEFT

1 Start with four cords. To work this onto a split ring, fold two lengths of cord in half and attach each to a split ring using a Lark's Head Knot (see page 10) to give you four working cords.

2 Using the second cord from the left, take it behind the left-hand "filler" cord, then over the filler cord and up through the loop.

3 Now take it over the filler cord again, up through the second loop, as shown, and pull tight.

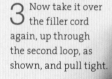

4 Using the third cord from the left, repeat the pattern of Steps 2–3, still wrapping over the same cord.

5 Using the right-hand cord, repeat the pattern of Steps 2–3. Keep knotting, repeating Steps 2–5, now using the new left-hand cord as the "filler."

DOUBLE HALF HITCH KNOT RIGHT

1 Start with four cords. To work this onto a split ring, fold two lengths of cord in half and attach each to a split ring using a Lark's Head Knot (see page 10) to give you four working cords.

2 Using the second cord from the right, take it behind the right-hand "filler" cord, then over the filler cord and up through the loop.

3 Now take it over the filler cord again, up through the second loop, as shown, and pull tight.

4 Using the third cord from the right, repeat the pattern of Steps 2–3, still wrapping over the same cord.

5 Using the left-hand cord, repeat the pattern of Steps 2–3. Keep knotting, repeating Steps 2–5, now using the new right-hand cord as the "filler."

Basic Tools

In some cultures, particularly Korean, all macramé knots were traditionally tied purely with the hands, with no other tools to aid tying. However, knotted jewelry is easier to make with a little help, even if it is simply a pin for attaching the end of your braiding to an anchor point.

When choosing materials and equipment to aid your knotted jewelry-making, choose the best you can afford. Good-quality equipment will last longer and make tying knots both easier and more efficient. Don't be tempted to struggle tying complex knots without the help of at least a macramé board and pins. You will only end up with a tangled mess, disheartened, and quite likely turned off tying knots forever!

One of the best aspects of creating jewelry with ornamental knots is the simplicity and lack of specialized equipment that's required. Most of the items described here can be purchased from craft, notions, or hardware stores, so are very easy to get hold of. Anything you cannot find locally will be available to buy on the Internet.

Essential Toolkit

Not many tools are actually essential for making macramé items, but the two essential items you will need are a macramé board and some pins, along with a few little sundry items.

Macramé board (1)

First and foremost, a suitable board is required to carry out your work. It's not ideal to work on a table or on your knee, and the work needs to be held firmly in place. A specially designed macramé board is available from selected bead and craft retailers. It's made from a soft, rubber-like material, and designed with cut-out notches around the edges to help you manage your cords. It also helps you keep the tension consistent.

Another option here is to use a plain corkboard, available from many stationery outlets and even some hardware stores. Letter size (A4 size) is probably the best to get so that you can accommodate your work easily. You can also make your own board by wrapping some soft quilting material around a clipboard and securing it at the back. I personally prefer either a corkboard or macramé board.

Pins

These essential little helpers will keep your work secure and the tension correct. I like to use standard-head pins. These can be purchased individually from most stationers or very often come with a corkboard. Other pins include specially designed long-shank pins (2) that are tailored for use with a macramé board.

Other Sundry Items

There are lots of tools available that will assist you in jewelry making. Read on to learn more about how each one can make your life a little easier and help you to get the best finished jewelry project.

Scissors (3)

Essential for cutting your thread, you can use a basic pair of scissors but you will find that a small, sharp pair will enable you to cut your threads closer to your work, giving you a neater finish. Only use your cord-cutting scissors for cutting cord. You will leave a sticky residue on them if you use them to cut sticky tape and this will stop cords from cutting cleanly in the future.

Thread cutters (4)

These can be worn around the neck and keep sharp blades at a safe distance from your fingers.

Pliers (5)

There is a huge variety of pliers on the market. You'll need to keep a small pair of needle-nose pliers at hand to attach findings, and open and close jump rings.

Craft glue

Craft glue should be diluted one part glue to 10 parts water, and then applied to stiffen large, open knots. It can also be used undiluted to seal cord ends. Apply with a paintbrush.

Sticky tape (6)

Sticky tape—either masking tape or clear tape—is really useful for keeping cords in place as you work, and can also be used to seal cord ends before knotting.

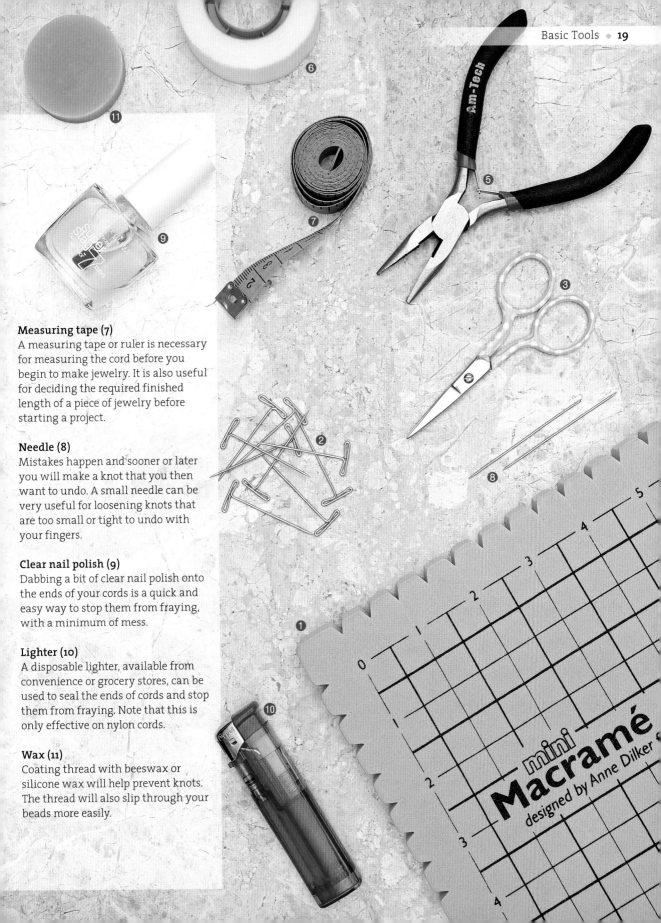

Measuring tape (7)
A measuring tape or ruler is necessary for measuring the cord before you begin to make jewelry. It is also useful for deciding the required finished length of a piece of jewelry before starting a project.

Needle (8)
Mistakes happen and sooner or later you will make a knot that you then want to undo. A small needle can be very useful for loosening knots that are too small or tight to undo with your fingers.

Clear nail polish (9)
Dabbing a bit of clear nail polish onto the ends of your cords is a quick and easy way to stop them from fraying, with a minimum of mess.

Lighter (10)
A disposable lighter, available from convenience or grocery stores, can be used to seal the ends of cords and stop them from fraying. Note that this is only effective on nylon cords.

Wax (11)
Coating thread with beeswax or silicone wax will help prevent knots. The thread will also slip through your beads more easily.

Cord widths

Cords come in many different widths, so you should bear this in mind before embarking on a project, especially if you are using beads, as you'll need to ensure the cord fits through the bead holes. Fine cords are well suited for making knotted jewelry—and will be the ones you use most for micro-macramé pieces—while thicker cords are perfect for making larger statement pieces.

0.5 mm

1 mm

1.5 mm

2 mm

2.5 mm

3 mm

3.5 mm

4 mm

Choosing Cords

Cord is the most important material for creating knotted jewelry—often it is the only material required. So take your time and learn what's available before you begin.

There is a huge range of cords to choose from, so you will be spoiled for choice. The majority of the projects in this book are made with micro-macramé cord, but there are also other cords available that you may like to try too.

When choosing cords for a macramé project, you need to take into consideration the actual size you want the finished project to be. A thin 0.5-mm cord will give you a delicate friendship bracelet. It is also the best cord to use when following an intricate pattern. In fact, a 0.5-mm cord is probably the most popular choice for most micro-macramé projects. It is also the only size of cord that will fit through a size 11 seed bead hole, so you will need to bear this in mind when choosing beads as well. A slightly thicker 1.5- or 2-mm cord would be a good choice for a man's bracelet or cuff, but would be unsuitable for a delicate pair of earrings, for example.

Of course, thickness is not the only thing to look out for when making your cord selection; there are also lots of different materials available. Specially made macramé cords are far more forgiving when it comes to unpicking knots—trying to unpick silk cords or hemp is not as easy to do. So, if you're a novice, micro-macramé cords would be best for you initially. Hemp is a wonderful choice if you like natural fibers, but it doesn't always have as many color choices as a lot of other cord types. It also has natural variations in the cord itself, and this can make your work look untidy if the project is intricate. It isn't always as smooth when you are threading on beads either.

Another important point to remember when selecting cords is that if you prefer to singe the ends of your cords to prevent fraying, this only works with nylon cords and not with cotton or hemp.

How much cord do I need?

Estimating quantities is something that comes with practice, and you will learn from experience, but here are a few rules of thumb to help you on your way.

The amounts of cord needed for the projects may appear to be an awful lot more than you might think. This is for a couple of reasons: First, the various knots use up a lot of cord in their creation; second, you actually need the extra length to work with and for you to be able to make the knots. It is no use if you have the exact amount of cord for your bracelet, necklace, or earrings, but no cord left to handle the projects and make the knots etc. It can be very frustrating if you are close to finishing a project, only to find that you are running short on cord, and either have to abandon the project or find some way of attaching more cord to be able to finish it—that is not always an easy or tidy job to do. It is much safer to start with a lot of cord and give yourself something to work with.

You can usually roughly estimate the lengths of cord required as follows:
- **Earrings:** 24 in. (61 cm) per pair
- **Bracelet:** 60 in. (1.5 m)
- **Necklace:** 150 in. (3.8 m)

These estimates are for designs that ask you to fold your cords in half when starting the project, so each cord becomes two working cords. If the pattern does not ask you to do this, you will more than likely need to double these amounts. Remember that these are just estimates and the amount of cord you will need depends on your design and the knots you choose to use. Some knots take much more cord to create than others. For example, a Double Half Hitch Knot takes up more cord than a Square Knot. Use the cord requirements listed at the beginning of each project as a guide.

Micro-macramé cord (1)
Micro-macramé cords come in a wide variety of colors. It is usually 18 gauge Nylon cord, which is strong and durable. It is approximately 0.5 mm thick—ideal when threading small seed beads—but can be purchased in thinner and wider diameters, too. C-lon and S-lon are popular brands, but in the materials listings in this book, we use micro-macramé cord as a general term.

Hemp (2) or jute (3)
Hemp is a natural fiber and is, therefore, a nice cord to combine with semiprecious beads to create jewelry that has a natural, "eco-friendly" look. It ties and tightens easily, but is too pliable for large, ornamental knots with loops, as it will not hold the loops. It is available in 0.5-mm and 1-mm widths in a wide variety of colors, though it suits pastel and neutral shades best. The same applies to jute, which is often sold as garden twine, although it is a little hairy.

Embroidery thread (4)
Embroidery thread is a 6- or 8-ply cord that is about 1 mm thick and comes in a massive range of colors, including variegated and metallic. It can be doubled up and plaited or braided, but isn't suitable for much more than that because the knots created are just too small to see!

Cotton (5)
Cotton cord is waxed and available in a range of diameters, from 0.5 mm up to 3 mm. As this is a natural cord, it looks good in neutral colors but is available in a small selection of brighter colors too. Use cotton cord for tying simpler knots, particularly plaits or braids, and combining with beads. It doesn't stretch and tightens well, but withstands only moderate manipulation.

Buying Beads

Ornamental knots are beautiful in themselves and some knotted jewelry is complete with just knots, however, the inclusion of beads can make an excellent addition. When choosing beads for your project the world is your oyster as there are so many to choose from, not only designs and colors but also sizes.

When choosing beads for your knotted jewelry, make sure they suit your project; in general, for fine micro-macramé pieces, you should opt for delicate beads. Large, fancy beads and even buttons can be used as focal centers. In fact, buttons make great alternatives to beads, just as long as they have a shank at the back that is large enough to thread your cords though rather than the traditional two holes.

If you're using a natural cord in neutral colors, such as hemp, use a natural-looking bead, like a semiprecious stone, rather than a bright, plastic bead. Also, match the beads to the knots. Lots of large beads with complex knots can look a bit overcrowded, so pair complicated knots with delicate beads, or a large beautiful pendant with simple knots.

Beads are available from local craft stores, online, and also specialized bead fairs, which are great to visit if there is one in your area. Look out for handmade beads because these will create a truly original piece of jewelry when teamed with hand-tied knots.

Seed Beads (1)

"Seed bead" is the name given to the smallest type of glass bead. They are generally under 1/5 in. (4 mm) in size

and shaped like a donut. Seed beads are the most commonly used beads in complex micro-macramé designs. Not all seed beads are the same, however. Once you start buying and using them, you'll soon notice a difference in size, shape, and quality between country of origin, manufacturer, and even individual colors. All of these add up to making the difference between an even, professional finish and an uneven, more freeform one. While either result is great in context, you want to make sure you get the one you want.

Sizes

Seed beads are sold by size, ranging from around size 22 and smaller, up to size 6, with the most common sizes being 15, 11, 8, and 6. As the bead size number increases, the physical size of each bead decreases. This is because the numbers are based on the "aught" sizing system, which originally specified how many beads fit onto a given thread. So, for example, a size 15 is a lot smaller than a size 6. You can buy seed beads individually, on strands, by weight, or by count. The most popular size of beads for a friendship-style bracelet is either size 11 or 8, but you should always check the cords against the size of the bead

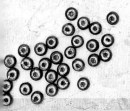

How many beads do I need?

Bead (approximate size)	Beads per 1 in. (2.5 cm)	Beads per 18 in. (46 cm)	Beads per 24 in. (61 cm)
Size 15 seed bead (1.5 mm)	17	307	401
Size 11 seed bead (1.8–2.2 mm)	12–14	210–256	278–339
Size 8 seed bead (3 mm)	8	140	185
Size 6 seed bead (4 mm)	6	115	153

You can't really estimate how many beads you will need for a bracelet or necklace, but it can normally be said that the smaller the bead, the more you will need.

The number of beads you need will vary radically according to which pattern you choose, and also the finished length of the project. You'll find that the size of seed

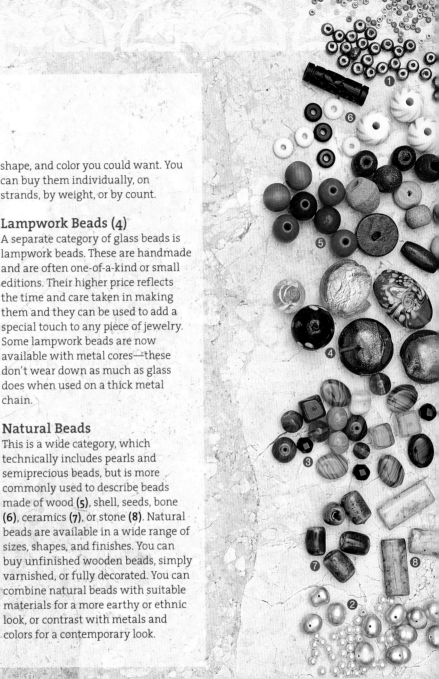

hole to make sure you can thread the cords through your selection of beads. This is a common error for a lot of people when choosing materials.

Pearls (2)

Eternally popular, and no longer just for your grandmother's single strand, pearls are now widely available and, more importantly, affordable. Make sure you know what you're buying first, though, as it's not always easy to tell the real thing from glass or plastic.

Identifying real pearls

A strand of real pearls will never contain identical-looking beads. There will be slight variations in color, shape, and size that don't happen with fake pearls. Furthermore, the surface of a real pearl won't be as smooth as that of a fake one. You may be able to identify this by sight and touch, or even by rubbing it on the surface of your teeth! If the outer coating peels away, the pearl may be a fake.

Glass Beads (3)

The most common and easy-to-find beads are those made of glass. They're made all over the world, using many different techniques, and are available in just about every size,

shape, and color you could want. You can buy them individually, on strands, by weight, or by count.

Lampwork Beads (4)

A separate category of glass beads is lampwork beads. These are handmade and are often one-of-a-kind or small editions. Their higher price reflects the time and care taken in making them and they can be used to add a special touch to any piece of jewelry. Some lampwork beads are now available with metal cores—these don't wear down as much as glass does when used on a thick metal chain.

Natural Beads

This is a wide category, which technically includes pearls and semiprecious beads, but is more commonly used to describe beads made of wood (5), shell, seeds, bone (6), ceramics (7), or stone (8). Natural beads are available in a wide range of sizes, shapes, and finishes. You can buy unfinished wooden beads, simply varnished, or fully decorated. You can combine natural beads with suitable materials for a more earthy or ethnic look, or contrast with metals and colors for a contemporary look.

Bead sizes

beads varies according to manufacturer, the finish on the bead, and even the color of the bead. However, the bead guide on the left shows an approximation of the average sizes and quantities, and may help when you start creating your own designs.

This table below shows the vital statistics of common bead sizes to give you an idea of the physical size of each and the number of beads per gram.

Seed bead size	Approximate size	Number per 1 gram	Number per 10 grams	Number per 100 grams
Size 15	1.5 mm	250	2,500	25,000
Size 11	2.2 mm	120	1,200	12,000
Size 8	3 mm	36	360	3,600
Size 6	4 mm	18	180	1,800

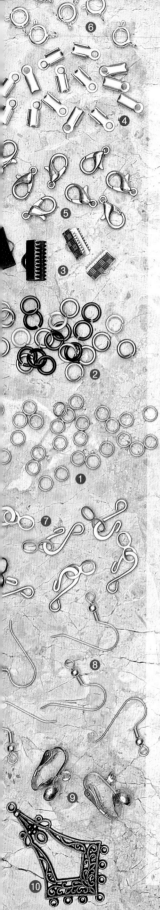

Findings

Findings are those little pieces, usually made of metal, that enable you to finish off your jewelry, make your life as a jeweler easier, and help you to create professional, attractive, and practical pieces.

It's important to choose findings that suit your jewelry: Delicate clasps often look better with fine micro-macramé cords. Make sure that the holes for fitting the clasps are large enough to fit your cord through and that the metal of the clasp suits the colors of the cords you are using. Cool colors, such as blue and purple, look stylish with silver findings, whereas gold suits warm oranges and reds. Findings are available from local craft stores and online. Look for something different to add originality to your jewelry.

Split and Jump Rings
Both these metal rings can be used to attach other findings to your jewelry.

Split rings (1)
These coils of metal (like a keyring) can be tricky to open, but cannot be pulled apart, so are really secure. Most projects in this book start by attaching cords to a split ring. The reason for using split rings rather than jump rings is because, if a cord can find a way to slip through the opening of a jump ring, then it normally does, but it can't with a split ring.

Jump rings (2)
These are small rings of metal

that are a lot easier to open and close than split rings, but can be pulled apart, so are less secure. Their ease of opening and closing makes them perfect for attaching findings to finish your jewelry pieces.

End Clamps
End clamps come in many different shapes and widths, and are an easy way to finish most bracelets and necklaces. Ribbon clamps (3) are solid, with teeth to grip your cords, while fold-over cord ends (4) can be crushed to hold the cord in place. End clamps often have a loop at the end that can be used to attach a clasp or another finding.

Fasteners
There is a huge range of clasps available for jewelry-making and the clasps you use will depend on what you have available, what the wearer finds easiest to use, and what suits your design.

Lobster clasps (5)
A good starting-point and a popular fastener—they are easy to use and have been used in many projects in this book. They can be attached to a jump or split ring, or even a strung, beaded loop on your jewelry. Choose a size and metal to match your work.

Bolt rings (6)
Secure, unobtrusive, and easy to fasten and open, but often quite small, so some people may struggle with them.

Hook clasps (7)
These are easy to fasten, which makes them ideal for necklaces, but can come undone more easily when used on bracelets so may not be suitable.

Earring Findings
With so many different earring findings now available, it can be hard to know where to start. They are largely interchangeable, so make your choice based on your personal preference.

Fish hooks (8)
The most common (and practical) earring findings can be found in many sizes, and some are now available with extra beads and other decorations built into them.

Clip-on earring findings (9)
These findings are often very tight when worn. Try to choose some that screw on, are looser, or contain soft pads to protect your ears.

Chandeliers (10)
Ideal for making earrings with more of a "wow factor."

Essential Skills

Although you do not need a lot of complex jewelry-making techniques to create beautiful micro-macramé work, it is useful to grasp just a few basic skills so that you can achieve the best look possible.

Macramé Boards

A macramé board is a specialist tool that has been specifically designed for making macramé and micro-macramé projects. It has a well-thought-out design that helps you keep your work neat and tidy. More importantly, it helps you keep your tension consistent and manage your cords. You will find that there is enough room on your board to hold several projects at the same time.

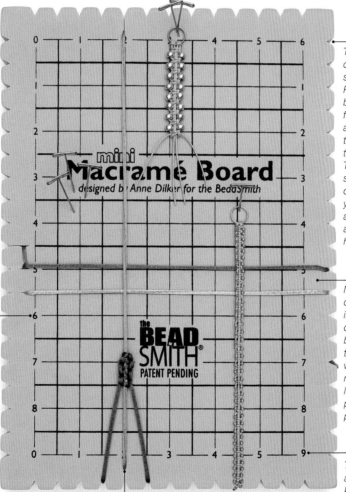

The notches around the outside of the board make securing your cords a breeze. Place the cord into a notch, bring the end around to the front through the next notch, and bring the end underneath the long cord, and then back through the original notch. This cord will now be really secure. Alternatively, tie a double knot in the end of your cord and then place it in a notch. The knot will catch at the back of the board and hold the cord in place.

The grid is marked out in inches and half-inches, which makes it really easy to measure your jewelry piece to the correct length and ensure that the width is consistent, and the starting and ending lengths equal.

Macramé boards are made of memory foam, which is "self-healing." So, if you choose to use pins on your board for added security, then any holes they leave will disappear as if by magic. Specially designed, long-shanked pins can be purchased, although any pins will do.

Alternatives to boards

Push pins and a corkboard can be an alternative to a macramé board, or you can make your own board with just a few simple steps using a clipboard, a few pins, and a little quilting.

You may find it helps to secure some cords at the bottom of the board as well. For example, if you secure the inner cords of a Square Knot by placing them through one of the bottom notches, they will stay in place perfectly as you work the outer cords around them and it will be much easier for you to continue with your work.

The numerical measures will also let you know how many knots it takes to make an inch or half-inch etc. in that particular cord. This will help you to be much more precise in your work and enable you to create a professionally finished piece.

Finishing a Project

There are many different ways to start or finish a project. Most of the projects in this book finish by attaching an end clamp and then a jump ring, as this is one of the easiest ways, but there are many more options you can try.

Attaching end clamps

End clamps, which are also sometimes called ribbon clamps, crimps, or cord ends, come in many different shapes and sizes. These little metal pieces are perfect for finishing off your cords, ribbons, or yarns. For the projects in this book, you will be working with multiple very fine cord ends, but it's a good idea to practice attaching an end clamp to just one slightly thicker cord first until you get the hang of it. Here we demonstrate with a fold-over cord end.

1 Place one end of your cord in the finding. You may find it easier to have some cord overlapping that you can trim off later. Using a pair of pliers that are flat inside, press in one side of the finding so that it holds the cord in place.

2 Press the other side of the finding in so that it lies on top of the first. It is very hard to get a neat finish at first, but you will improve with practice. The aim at first is simply to secure the cord.

3 Now you know what you're doing, you can easily secure multiple cord ends in one ribbon/end clasp. Simply place them all in the finding at the same time and close to secure.

Attaching jump rings

Once you've secured your cord ends with an end clamp, attach a jump ring so that you can secure the fastening. Why not also attach a jump ring to the starting split ring of your project for symmetry.

1 Hold the jump ring on either side of the opening using two pairs of pliers.

2 Do not pull the ring apart, as this will distort the shape and the ring will not close properly again. Use one pair of pliers to hold the jump ring and the other to push the other half of the ring backward.

3 Thread the end clamp and, if applicable, fastening—for example, a lobster clasp—onto the open jump ring, then move the pliers in the opposite directions to close the ring.

Finishing with Lark's Head Knots

If you are a little more advanced in your macramé knotting techniques, you can finish a project by attaching the cords to a split ring using Lark's Head Knots. This does require a little practice, but is easier if you turn your work upside down first.

1 Attach your innermost cords to the split ring with a Lark's Head Knot (see page 10) first and then work outward.

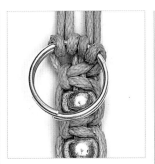

2 After you have attached all of the cords in this way, you need to pull them very tightly, and then snip off the excess cords to leave just a couple of millimeters.

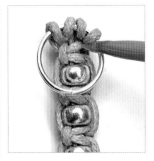

3 Dab a little clear craft glue on the knots to keep everything in place and prevent the knots from coming undone. (See the Lacy Earrings on pages 102–106 for some illustrated examples.)

Finishing friendship bracelets

You can tie together some smaller and more delicate friendship bracelets using a single knot. Simply start and finish these types of bracelets by tying the start and end of the bracelet with an Overhand Knot (see page 11), then leave approximately 5–6 in. (13–15 cm) or so of extra cord loose for tying the bracelet around the wrist. You can also braid the end cords to create a more pleasing finish, and then secure with a small Overhand Knot.

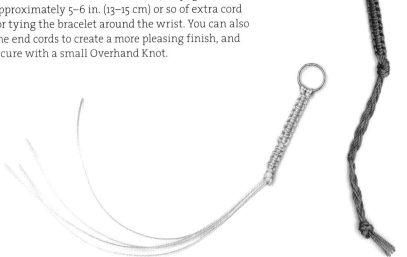

Experiment with finishes

- There are lots of wonderful little toggles and fasteners out there that you could use for attaching your cords, instead of a split ring. Many different designs are available at most good bead retailers.

- Another option for a finished bracelet is to use a button at one end and make a buttonhole at the other, either using Square Knots or just by creating a loop.

Designing with Color

We usually notice the color of a piece of jewelry first: We notice if it's bright or subtle, if it contrasts or blends with what someone is wearing, or matches the silver or gold metal clasp used in the design.

Color also helps us to identify what the beads are made of, if the piece was intended to make a statement, and if so, what? Color often has meaning and purpose, but remember that color can be played with and that, ultimately, it comes down to personal taste.

Starting Out With Color
Some people put colors together without even thinking about it, whereas others need to work hard to get a result they're happy with. If you fall into the second category, don't worry—there are lots of tips and tricks to help you find a combination you're happy with. First, let's learn more about color.

Color Wheels
The best tool to help you understand color is a color wheel. This shows all the primary (red, yellow, blue) and secondary (green, orange, violet) colors. The position of

each color on the wheel determines how it reacts with others. Colors opposite each other are called complementary colors. They create striking contrasts when placed side by side.

Finding the Right Color Combination
There are set color combinations and theories on combining different colors, the rules of which can help you to make informed choices. Practice with a specific bead and follow the rules to see what combinations you can come up with that appeal to you.

Choose a Starting Color
On the right, we show how you can build some color schemes based around a central color—in this case, orange. Orange is a very strong color that most people shy away from using since they don't know where to begin with it, but it is perfect for experimenting with.

Primary colors
These are the main colors: Blue, yellow, and red. They are called primary colors because they cannot be made from any other colors—they are pure color.

Secondary colors
These are colors made when you mix the primaries: Green (from yellow and blue); violet (from red and blue); and orange (from red and yellow).

RULES ARE MADE TO BE BROKEN
Don't forget that although color rules are there to help you, they can also be broken. A complete mix of colors can work—and look fantastic.

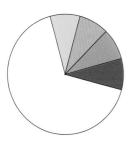

Analogous color schemes

These schemes use two or more colors that sit next to each other on the color wheel. Here, this means matching the orange beads with yellows, and reds with oranges, all of which work together to tone down the bright orange.

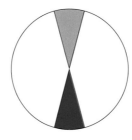

Complementary colors

Often also called contrasting colors, these work according to the theory that the colors sitting opposite each other on the color wheel work well together—red and green, yellow and violet, and, in this case, orange and blue. In complementary combinations both colors work with each other: The result is that the orange and blue beads both look very strong.

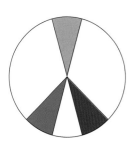

Split-complementary

This approach involves combining your first color with the two colors that sit on either side of its complementary. In this case, it means using green and violet beads in combination with the original orange ones. See how the orange is toned down by the combination.

ADDING COLORS IN OTHER WAYS

It's not just beads that can be used to create the color combinations you want. Remember that the cord you use, as well as any metal findings you choose, should all be taken into account when designing your pieces of jewelry.

Black and white

Although technically not colors, black and white are often put in the primary color category, as they are basic colors that are used to enhance others.

Visual Contents

44

Cluster of Pearls Necklace

46

Disco Bead Bracelet

48

Multi-Stranded
Necklace

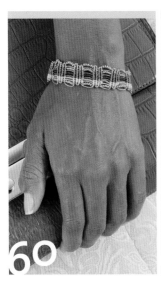

60

**Intermediate
Projects**
Striped Beaded Bracelet

64

Beaded Bracelet with
Focal Center

66

Simple Tassel Earrings

69

Owl Pendant

72

76

78

99

102

107

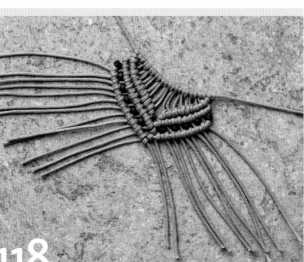

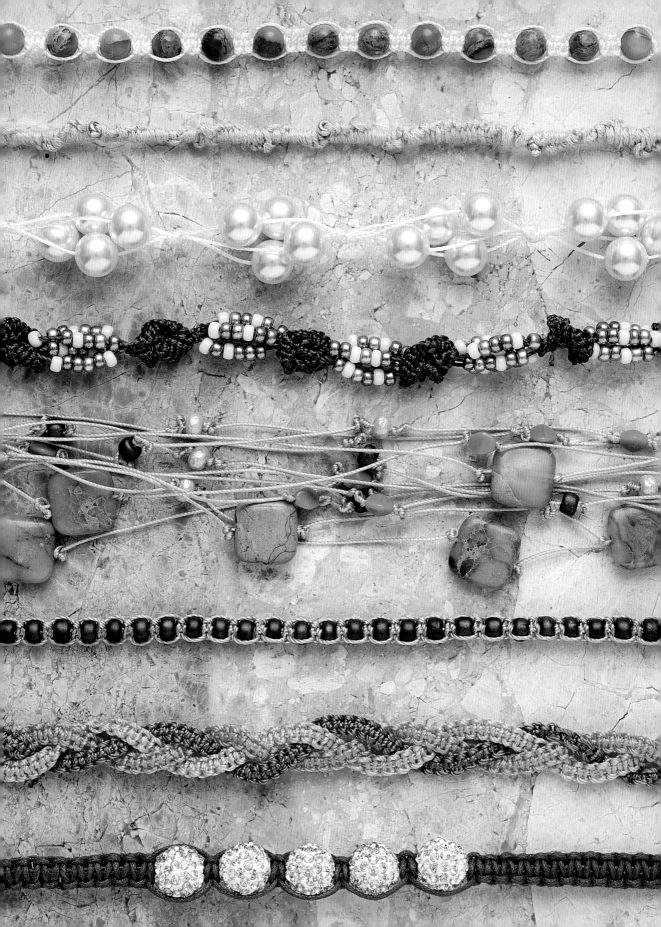

2

Beginner Projects

The following ten projects are perfect for beginner macramé jewelers. Through these simple yet striking pieces, you will learn the core knots, start working with beads, and your confidence will soar.

Simple Beaded Friendship Bracelet

This fashionable little friendship bracelet is quick and easy to make. You can wear it alone or make several in complementary colors and wear them together.

YOU WILL NEED:

- 2 lengths of micro-macramé cord, measuring approx. 60 in. (152 cm)
- Approx. 90 size 11 seed beads
- 1 x 10 mm split ring
- 1 x fold-over cord end
- 1 x 6 mm jump ring
- 1 x lobster clasp
- Needle-nose pliers

SKILL LEVEL: EASY

Dimensions
- Length: 7½ in. (19 cm)
- Width: ¼ in. (6 mm)

Knot Finder
- Lark's Head Knot, see page 10
- Square Knot, see page 12

1 Fold the two cords in half and attach them individually to the split ring using Lark's Head Knots (see page 10). You now have a total of four cords to work with—two inner and two outer cords.

2 Using the two outer cords, tie a complete Square Knot by wrapping them around the two inner cords (see page 12).

Light fantastic
An easy project for beginners—there is fun to be had in choosing colors and beads that catch the light.

3 Thread one seed bead onto each of the outer cords.

4 Repeat Steps 2 and 3 until the bracelet measures approximately 7 in. (18 cm) or the desired length for your wrist. To finish, secure the ends of the cords in a fold-over cord end, and then attach a jump ring and lobster clasp for fastening the bracelet (see Finishing a Project, page 26).

Mermaid Wrap Bracelet

This pretty and dainty wrap bracelet is made from swirling knots and accented with silver beads. It's super-quick to make, too.

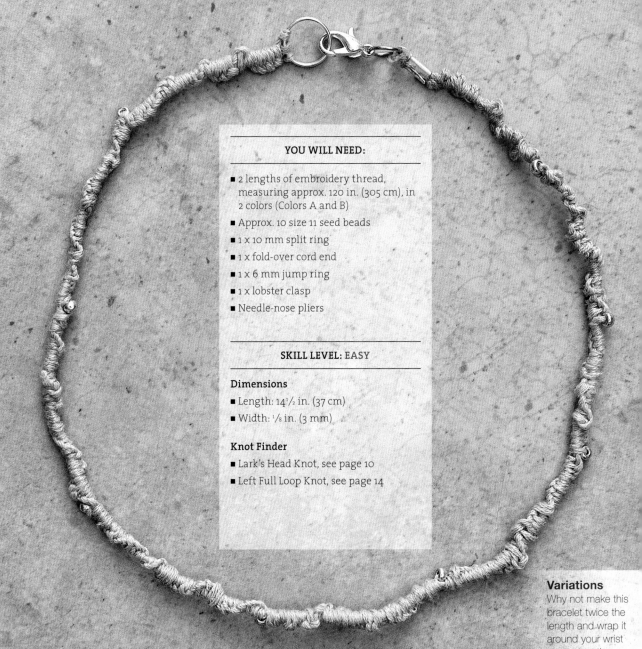

YOU WILL NEED:

- 2 lengths of embroidery thread, measuring approx. 120 in. (305 cm), in 2 colors (Colors A and B)
- Approx. 10 size 11 seed beads
- 1 x 10 mm split ring
- 1 x fold-over cord end
- 1 x 6 mm jump ring
- 1 x lobster clasp
- Needle-nose pliers

SKILL LEVEL: EASY

Dimensions
- Length: 14$\frac{1}{2}$ in. (37 cm)
- Width: $\frac{1}{8}$ in. (3 mm)

Knot Finder
- Lark's Head Knot, see page 10
- Left Full Loop Knot, see page 14

Variations
Why not make this bracelet twice the length and wrap it around your wrist even more times.

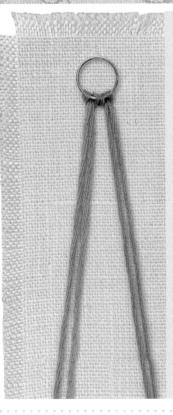

1 Fold the two cords in half and attach them individually to the split ring using Lark's Head Knots (see page 10). You now have a total of four cords to work with—two inner and two outer cords.

2 Using just one strand of Color A, make a series of Left Full Loop Knots (see page 14) around the other three cords until your work measures approximately 2 in. (5 cm) in length. Then thread one bead onto your working cord and tie one last Left Full Loop Knot around the other cords to secure the bead.

3 Repeat Step 2, but this time take a strand of Color B, wrap it around the other cords using a series of Left Full Loop Knots for another 2 in. (5 cm), and then attach another bead as in Step 2.

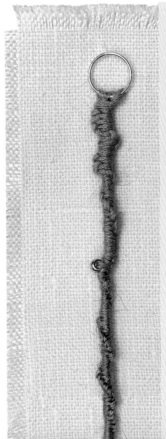

4 Repeat Steps 2 and 3 until the bracelet measures around 14 in. (36 cm) or is long enough to wrap around your wrist twice. To finish, secure the ends of the cords in a fold-over cord end, and attach a jump ring and lobster clasp for fastening the bracelet (see Finishing a Project, page 26). You can also add an optional charm to the jump ring at this stage.

A matching set
Why not make two? Wrap one three times around your wrist as a bracelet, and wear the other as a matching necklace.

YOU WILL NEED:

- 2 lengths of micro-macramé cord, measuring approx. 180 in. (457 cm)
- Approx. 110 size 8 seed beads
- 1 x 10 mm split ring
- 1 x fold-over cord end
- 1 x 6 mm jump ring
- 1 x lobster clasp
- Needle-nose pliers

SKILL LEVEL: EASY

Dimensions
- Length: $21^{1}/_{2}$ in. (54.5 cm)
- Width: $^{1}/_{8}$ in. (3 mm)

Knot Finder
- Lark's Head Knot, see page 10
- Square Knot, see page 12

This very attractive wrap bracelet is simple to make and so versatile that it can also be worn as a necklace.

Beaded Triple Wrap Bracelet

1 Fold the two cords in half and attach them individually to the split ring using Lark's Head Knots (see page 10). You now have a total of four cords to work with—two inner and two outer cords.

2 Using the two outer cords, tie a Square Knot by wrapping them around the two inner cords (see page 12).

3 Take the two inner cords and thread them both through a seed bead.

4 Repeat Steps 2 and 3 until the bracelet measures around 21 in. (53 cm) or will wrap around your wrist three times. To finish, secure the ends of the cords in a fold-over cord end, and attach a jump ring and lobster clasp for fastening the bracelet (see Finishing a Project, page 26).

Braided Bracelet

Take your braiding to a higher level with this wonderful friendship-style bracelet that is very simple to make. There are no beads in this bracelet—just knots and braids.

YOU WILL NEED:

- 2 lengths of micro-macramé cord, measuring approx. 90 in. (229 cm), in 3 colors (Colors A, B, and C)
- 1 x 10 mm split ring
- 1 x ribbon clamp
- 1 x 6 mm jump ring
- 1 x lobster clasp
- Needle-nose pliers

SKILL LEVEL: EASY

Dimensions
- Length: 7 3/4 in. (19.5 cm)
- Width: 3/8 in. (1 cm)

Knot Finder
- Lark's Head Knot, see page 10
- Square Knot, see page 12

Using color
Play around with using complementary and contrasting colors in your cord choice to achieve different looks.

1 Starting with Color A, fold the cords in half and attach them individually to the split ring using Lark's Head Knots (see page 10). You now have a total of four cords to work with—two inner and two outer cords.

2 Tie a series of Square Knots (see page 12) until the bracelet measures approximately 9 in. (23 cm) in length or about 2 in. (5 cm) longer than the length that you require.

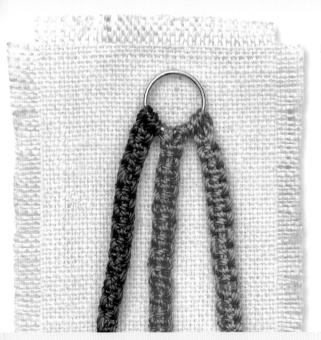

3 Repeat Steps 1 and 2 using Color B and then Color C, on either side of the Color A section.

4 Using all three pieces, work a simple braid by crossing the piece on the right over the middle piece, then crossing the left piece over the new middle piece. Continue to cross the right and left pieces over the middle piece until you reach the end of your cords. To finish, secure the ends of the cords in a ribbon clamp, and attach a jump ring and lobster clasp for fastening the bracelet (see Finishing a Project, page 26).

Cluster of Pearls Necklace

This is an outstandingly pretty necklace that will always be noticed and yet is so quick and easy to create using just a few small Overhand Knots.

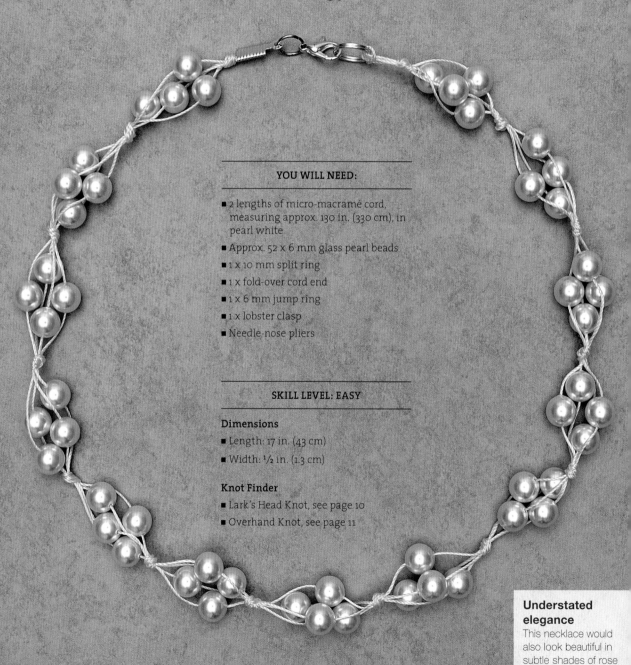

YOU WILL NEED:

- 2 lengths of micro-macramé cord, measuring approx. 130 in. (330 cm), in pearl white
- Approx. 52 x 6 mm glass pearl beads
- 1 x 10 mm split ring
- 1 x fold-over cord end
- 1 x 6 mm jump ring
- 1 x lobster clasp
- Needle-nose pliers

SKILL LEVEL: EASY

Dimensions
- Length: 17 in. (43 cm)
- Width: ½ in. (1.3 cm)

Knot Finder
- Lark's Head Knot, see page 10
- Overhand Knot, see page 11

Understated elegance
This necklace would also look beautiful in subtle shades of rose pink or soft lilac.

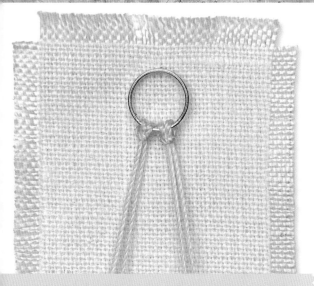

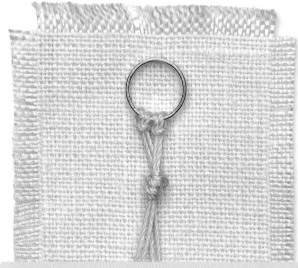

1 Fold the two cords in half and attach them individually to the split ring using Lark's Head Knots (see page 10). You now have a total of four cords to work with—two inner and two outer cords.

2 Use all four cords to create an Overhand Knot (see page 11).

3 Thread each of the four cords with a glass pearl bead, staggering them slightly to form a pleasing arrangement. Tie an Overhand Knot after placing the four glass pearl beads.

4 Repeat Steps 2 and 3 until your work measures approximately 16½ in. (42 cm) in length. To finish, secure the ends of the cords in a fold-over cord end, and attach a jump ring and lobster clasp for fastening the necklace (see Finishing a Project, page 26).

Metallic madness
The contrast of silver and blue makes this a real statement piece.

Disco Bead Bracelet

A chic, highly fashionable, and stylish bracelet with dazzling beads, which will brighten up any outfit. This is both easy to make and a real eye-catcher.

YOU WILL NEED:

- 2 lengths of 0.5 mm waxed cord, measuring approx. 60 in. (152 cm)
- 5 x 10 mm disco-style beads
- 1 x 10 mm split ring
- 1 x fold-over cord end
- 1 x 6 mm jump ring
- 1 x lobster clasp
- Needle-nose pliers

SKILL LEVEL: EASY

Dimensions
- Length: 7 in. (18 cm)
- Width: ³/₈ in. (1 cm)

Knot Finder
- Lark's Head Knot, see page 10
- Square Knot, see page 12

1 Fold the two cords in half and attach them individually to the split ring using Lark's Head Knots (see page 10). You now have a total of four cords to work with—two inner and two outer cords.

2 Tie a series of Square Knots (see page 12) until your work measures approximately 2 in. (5 cm) in length.

3 Take the two inner cords and thread them through one of the disco-style beads.

4 Create a Square Knot and then thread another bead through the two inner cords as in Step 3. Repeat, making one Square Knot and threading on one bead until all five beads have been used. Then repeat Step 2 until the second series of Square Knots also measures 2 in. (5 cm). To finish, secure the ends of the cords in a fold-over cord end, and attach a jump ring and lobster clasp for fastening the bracelet (see Finishing a Project, page 26).

Multi-Stranded Necklace

This stunning statement necklace may look complex, but it's as easy as counting 1,2,3.

YOU WILL NEED:

- 6 lengths of micro-macramé cord, measuring approx. 50 in. (127 cm)
- Approx. 75 beads in various shapes, sizes, and colors
- 1 x 10 mm split ring
- 1 x fold-over cord end
- 1 x 6 mm jump ring
- 1 x lobster clasp
- Needle-nose pliers

SKILL LEVEL: EASY

Dimensions

- Length: 15¾ in. (40 cm)
- Width: ¾ in. (2 cm)

Knot Finder

- Lark's Head Knot, see page 10
- Overhand Knot, see page 11

Spikes of color
The neutral colored cords and beads used for most of the necklace really make the turquoise beads pop.

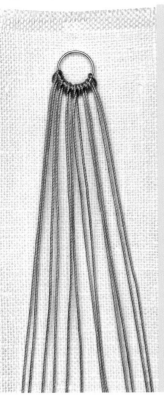

1 Fold the six cords in half and attach them individually to the split ring using Lark's Head Knots (see page 10). You now have a total of 12 cords to work with.

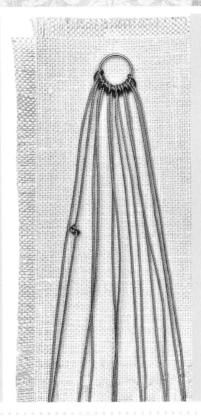

2 Work two Overhand Knots (see page 11) over the top of each other on one of the cords.

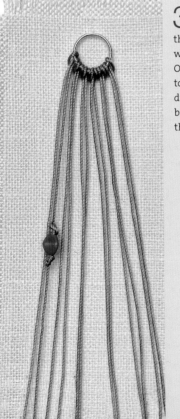

3 Thread one of your beads onto the cord and then work two more Overhand Knots on top of each other directly below the bead. This will keep the bead in place.

4 Repeat Steps 2 and 3 further down the cord, leaving about 2–3 in. (5–8 cm) between each bead. Repeat along the other 11 cords. Finish off the piece by securing the ends of the cords in a fold-over cord end, and attaching a jump ring and lobster clasp for fastening the necklace (see Finishing a Project, page 26).

Nautical Stripes Bracelet

This little bracelet is very easy to make and has the option of adding a themed button as a focal point. Choose your own theme, or keep it nautical but nice.

YOU WILL NEED:

- 3 lengths of embroidery thread, measuring approx. 100 in. (254 cm), in 3 colors
- 1 x nautical focal button, with a shank large enough to thread 6 cords through (optional)
- 1 x 10 mm split ring
- 1 x fold-over cord end
- 1 x 6 mm jump ring
- 1 x lobster clasp
- Needle-nose pliers

SKILL LEVEL: EASY

Dimensions

- Length: 7 in. (18 cm)
- Width: ½ in. (1.3 cm)

Knot Finder

- Lark's Head Knot, see page 10
- Left Full Loop Knot, see page 14

Simple and stylish
Leave out the button if you wish and instead create a bracelet with a lovely striped design.

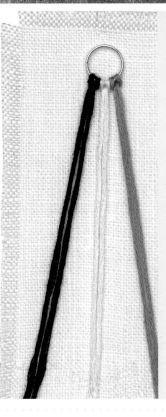

1 Fold the three cords in half and attach them individually to the split ring using Lark's Head Knots (page 10). You now have a total of six cords to work with.

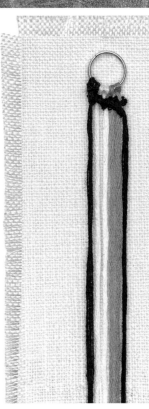

2 Using the thread on the far left-hand side of your project, work a series of Left Full Loop Knots (see page 14) over all the other threads.

3 Repeat Step 2, continuing to make a series of Left Full Loop Knots until your work measures approximately 3½ in. (9 cm) in length. Then thread all of the strands through the shank of the focal button.

4 Repeat Step 2 until your work measures approximately 6½ in. (16.5 cm) in length. Finish off the piece by securing the ends of the cords in a fold-over cord end, and attaching a jump ring and lobster clasp for fastening the bracelet (see Finishing a Project, page 26).

Jasper Bracelet

This lovely little bracelet is easy to make and light to wear. It looks beautiful in these natural earth tones.

YOU WILL NEED:

- 2 lengths of micro-macramé cord, measuring approx. 50 in. (127 cm)
- Approx. 16 x 6 mm jasper beads
- 1 x 10 mm split ring
- 1 x fold-over cord end
- 2 x 6 mm jump rings
- 1 x lobster clasp
- Needle-nose pliers

SKILL LEVEL: EASY

Dimensions
- Length: 7½ in. (19 cm)
- Width: ¼ in. (6 mm)

Knot Finder
- Lark's Head Knot, see page 10
- Square Knot, see page 12

A touch of nature
The color of these jasper beads and the lightness of the cord gives this bracelet a light and natural feel.

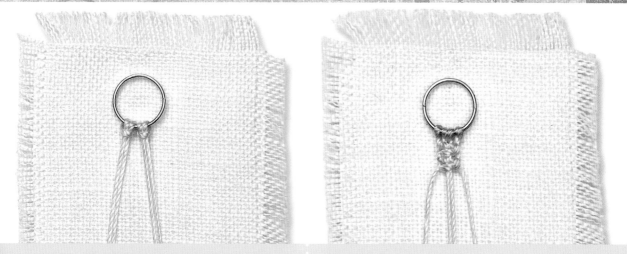

1 Fold the two cords in half and attach them individually to the split ring using Lark's Head Knots (see page 10). You now have a total of four cords to work with—two inner and two outer cords.

2 Tie two Square Knots (see page 12).

3 Thread the two inner cords through one of the jasper beads.

4 Repeat Steps 2–3 until your work measures approximately 7 in. (18 cm) in length or the desired length for your wrist. To finish, snip off the excess cords, secure the ends of the cords in a fold-over cord end, and attach jump rings and a lobster clasp for fastening the bracelet (see Finishing a Project, page 26).

Knotted Spiral Bracelet

This delightful little bracelet is easy to make with just a few twists and turns.

YOU WILL NEED:	SKILL LEVEL: EASY

YOU WILL NEED:

- 2 lengths of micro-macramé cord, measuring approx. 100 in. (254 cm)
- Approx. 120 size 8 seed beads in various colors
- 1 x 10 mm split ring
- 1 x fold-over cord end
- 2 x 6 mm jump rings
- 1 x lobster clasp
- Needle-nose pliers

SKILL LEVEL: EASY

Dimensions
- Length: 7 in. (18 cm)
- Width: ¼ in. (6 mm)

Knot Finder
- Lark's Head Knot, see page 10
- Spiral Knot, see page 13
- Overhand Knot, see page 11

NOTE: To make a necklace, begin with lengths of micro-macramé cord approximately 180 in. (457 cm) long.

1 Fold the two cords in half and attach them individually to the split ring using Lark's Head Knots (see page 10). You now have a total of four cords to work with—two inner and two outer cords.

2 Work a Spiral Knot (see page 13).

Twin set
A matching bracelet and necklace set would make a beautiful gift for a friend or loved one.

3 Continue to work a series of Spiral Knots until your bracelet measures approximately 1½ in. (3.8 cm) in length.

4 Tie one Overhand Knot (see page 11) with the Spiral knotted section of your work, as shown.

5 Thread six of the size 8 seed beads onto each cord, mixing up the colors randomly.

6 Tie one Overhand Knot using all of the cords.

Series of Spiral Knots
tied with an Overhand
Knot (Steps 2–4)

Mix up the colors of your
beads randomly, or stick
to a repeating pattern
(Step 5)

For a bracelet, keep
repeating until your
macramé measures approx.
6¼ in. (16.5 cm) long

7 Repeat Steps 2–6.

8 Continue repeating Steps 2–6 until your work reaches the
desired length for either a bracelet or necklace. To finish, snip
off any excess cords, secure the ends in a fold-over cord end, and
attach jump rings and a lobster clasp for fastening the piece (see
Finishing a Project, page 26).

3

Intermediate Projects

Slightly more intricate and time consuming than the Beginner Projects, the nine projects in this chapter will really help you develop your macramé skills. Working with multiple cords, colors, and beads, you will have to concentrate a bit more, but it will be worth it!

Fall colors
The matching beads and
cords in fall tones create a
harmonious look. Try beads in
contrasting colors, or a black
and white palette for something
completely different.

Striped Beaded Bracelet

A stripey little beaded affair. Let your imagination with colors loose
on this project and you will come up with a different look each time.

YOU WILL NEED:	SKILL LEVEL: INTERMEDIATE

YOU WILL NEED:

- 2 lengths of micro-macramé cord,
  measuring approx. 60 in. (152.5 cm), in
  3 colors (Colors A, B, and C)
- 4 lengths of micro-macramé cord,
  measuring approx. 60 in. (152.5 cm) in
  Color D
- Approx. 250 size 11 seed beads: 50 in
  Colors A, B, and C, and 100 in Color D
- 2 x ribbon clamps
- 2 x 6 mm jump rings
- 1 x lobster clasp
- Needle-nose pliers

SKILL LEVEL: INTERMEDIATE

Dimensions
- Length: 7$\frac{1}{2}$ in. (19 cm)
- Width: $\frac{3}{4}$ in. (2 cm)

Knot Finder
- Double Half Hitch Knot, see pages 16–17

1 Attach and enclose the cords in one of the ribbon clamps, as shown here. Make sure that you place the two lengths of Color D on the outside.

2 Starting with the cord on the far left, work a row of Double Half Hitch Knots (see pages 16–17) parallel to the ribbon clamp.

3 Starting with the cord on the far right, create another row of Double Half Hitch Knots.

4 Repeat Steps 2–3.

*Four rows of Double Half
Hitch Knots (Steps 2–4)*

*Thread five beads onto
every other cord (Step 5)*

*Mixing the colors of
the beads would create
a different look*

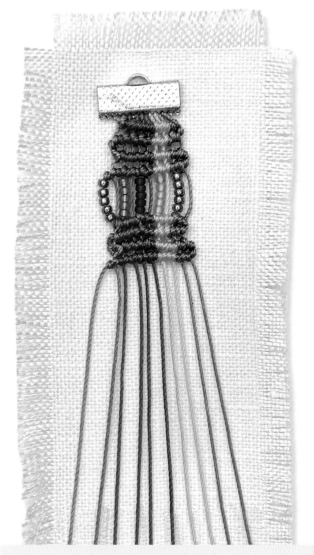

5 Starting from the left, thread the seed beads onto the cord
as follows: Five beads in Color D onto cord 1
Five beads in Color A onto cord 3
Five beads in Color B onto cord 5
Five beads in Color C onto cord 7
Five beads in Color D onto cord 9

6 Work another four rows of Double Half Hitch Knots as you did
in Steps 2 and 3.

Attach a jump ring and lobster clasp to fasten the bracelet (Step 7)

7 Repeat Steps 5 and 6 until your work measures approximately 7 in. (18 cm) in length or the desired length for your wrist. Snip off excess cords and attach the other ribbon clamp, jump rings, and a lobster clasp for fastening the bracelet (see Finishing a Project, page 26).

Beaded Bracelet with Focal Center

This classy bracelet is a must, with or without an optional centerpiece. It's a little more advanced than some of the easier projects, but get started with the Double Half Hitch Knot and you are ready to go.

YOU WILL NEED:

- 6 lengths of micro-macramé cord, measuring approx. 90 in. (229 cm)
- Approx. 90 size 11 seed beads
- Approx. 14 x 4 mm cube beads
- 1 x focal button with a shank large enough to thread 12 cords through (optional)
- 1 x 10 mm split ring
- 1 x ribbon clamp
- 1 x 6 mm jump ring
- 1 x lobster clasp
- Needle-nose pliers

SKILL LEVEL: INTERMEDIATE

Dimensions
- Length: 7$\frac{1}{2}$ in. (19 cm)
- Width: $\frac{3}{4}$ in. (2 cm)

Knot Finder
- Lark's Head Knot, see page 10
- Double Half Hitch Knot, see pages 16–17

Versatile style
The choice of focal button gives this bracelet a natural, beachy feel, but you could use any bead of your choice.

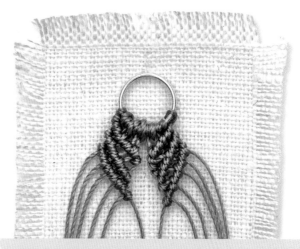

1 Fold the six cords in half and attach them individually to the split ring using Lark's Head Knots (see page 10). You now have a total of 12 cords to work with.

2 Using the first six cords on the left and starting from the outside, work three rows of diagonal Double Half Hitch Knots (see pages 16–17). Then repeat this process with the six cords on the right, again starting from the outside.

3 Take the two innermost cords and thread them both through a 4 mm cube bead. Then thread the other cords as follows: Starting with the outermost cord on the right, thread every other cord with a size 11 seed bead. Repeat with the cords on the left. At this stage, either repeat Steps 2 and 3 until the bracelet measures approximately 7 in. (18 cm) in length or the desired length for your wrist and then finish off, or continue to Step 4 now to add the focal button.

4 To add the focal center, repeat Steps 2 and 3 until your work measures approximately 3½ in. (9 cm) in length. Thread all of the cords through the focal button and then continue repeating Steps 2 and 3 until the bracelet measures 7 in. (18 cm) in length or the desired length for your wrist. To finish, place the ends of the cords in a ribbon clamp, and attach a jump ring and lobster clasp for fastening the bracelet (see Finishing a Project, page 26).

Simple Tassel Earrings

These pretty earrings are fairly easy to make and can be completed in very little time. The configuration of the larger central and smaller outer beads almost gives the impression of a butterfly.

YOU WILL NEED:

- 8 lengths of micro-macramé cord, measuring approx. 24 in. (61 cm)
- 2 x 6 mm focal beads
- 80 size 8 seed beads
- 2 x 10 mm split rings
- 2 x ear wires
- Needle-nose pliers

SKILL LEVEL: INTERMEDIATE

Dimensions (each)
- Length: 3¼ in. (8.5 cm)
- Width: 1 in. (2.5 cm)

Knot Finder
- Lark's Head Knot, see page 10
- Double Half Hitch Knot, see pages 16–17
- Overhand Knot, see page 11

A matching pair
It can be tricky to create two identical earrings. But don't beat yourself up too much—they'll never be worn side by side.

1 Fold four of the cords in half and attach them individually to one of the split rings using Lark's Head Knots (see page 10). You now have a total of eight cords to work with.

2 Using the first four cords on the left and starting from the outside, work two rows of Double Half Hitch Knots (see pages 16–17). Then repeat this process with the cords on the right, again starting from the outside.

3 Thread the two inner cords through one of the 6 mm focal beads.

4 Thread nine of the size 8 seed beads onto the cord on the far left, seven beads onto the next cord in, and four onto the next.

5 Starting with the fourth cord from the left, work two rows of Double Half Hitch Knots.

6 Repeat Steps 4 and 5 with the cords on the right, reversing the direction of the beads and knots.

7 Using all the cords, tie an Overhand Knot (see page 11).

8 Snip off the excess cord, leaving some tassels, and then repeat the process to create the second earring. To finish, attach the ear wires using pliers, as you would attach a jump ring (see Finishing a Project, page 26).

Owl Pendant

This is a wise and wonderful little creation that can be suspended from anything you wish.

YOU WILL NEED:

- 6 lengths of micro-macramé cord, measuring approx. 30 in. (76 cm)
- 2 x 4 mm focal beads
- 1 x 10 mm split ring

SKILL LEVEL: INTERMEDIATE

Dimensions
- Length: 2³/₄ in. (7 cm)
- Width: ³/₄ in. (2 cm)

Knot Finder
- Lark's Head Knot, see page 10
- Double Half Hitch Knot, see pages 16–17
- Right Full Loop Knot, see page 15
- Overhand Knot, page 11

Multiple uses
We've attached the owl pendant to a long, silver chain. But you could use anything you like. You could turn it into a keyring or a purse charm.

1 Fold the six cords in half and attach them individually to the split ring using Lark's Head Knots (see page 10). You now have a total of 12 cords to work with.

2 Using the first six cords on the left and starting from the outside, work two rows of diagonal Double Half Hitch Knots (see pages 16–17). Repeat this process with the six cords on the right, again starting from the outside. Then tie the two inner cords together using a Right Full Loop Knot (see page 15).

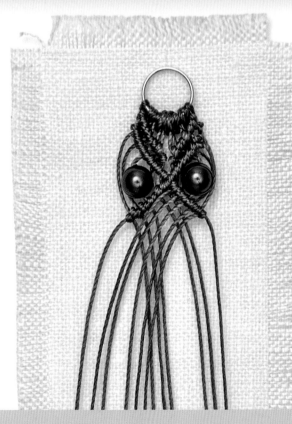

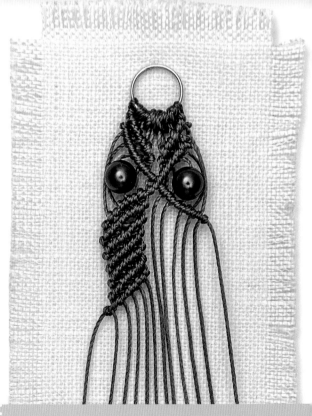

5 Starting with the sixth cord from the right, work a row of Double Half Hitch Knots to the right.

6 Starting with the sixth cord from the left, work another six rows of Double Half Hitch Knots, working right to left.

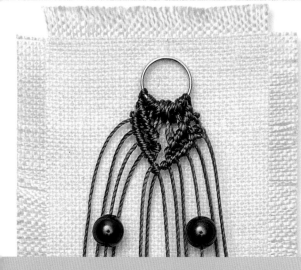

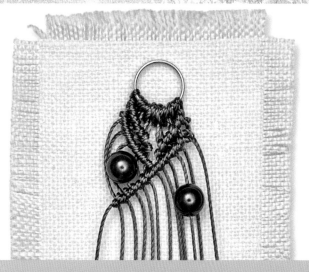

3 Thread one of the 4 mm focal beads through the third cord from the left and then thread the second bead through the third cord from the right.

4 Starting with the sixth cord from the left, work a row of Double Half Hitch Knots to the left.

7 Repeat Step 6 with the cords on the right, starting with the sixth cord from the right and working left to right.

8 Using all the cords, tie an Overhand Knot (see page 11). Then snip off the excess cord.

Wrap your favorite gemstone in this fashionable little gem case and suspend it from a complementary spiral necklace.

YOU WILL NEED:

- 2 lengths of micro-macramé cord, measuring approx. 160 in. (406 cm)
- 4 lengths of micro-macramé cord, measuring approx. 24 in. (61 cm)
- A gemstone of choice, measuring approx. 1¹⁄₂ in. (3.8 cm) in length
- 1 x 10 mm split ring
- 1 x fold-over cord end
- 1 x 6 mm jump ring
- 1 x lobster clasp
- Needle-nose pliers

SKILL LEVEL: INTERMEDIATE

Dimensions (necklace)
- Length: 19 in. (48.5 cm)
- Width: ¹⁄₈ in. (3 mm)

Knot Finder
- Lark's Head Knot, see page 10
- Spiral Knot, see page 13
- Overhand Knot, see page 11

Spiral Necklace with Netted Gem Case

1 To make the spiral necklace, fold the two longer lengths of cord in half and attach them individually to the split ring using Lark's Head Knots (see page 10). You now have a total of four cords to work with.

2 Tie a Spiral Knot—this is half of a Square Knot (see page 13).

5 Spread out the cords, take the sixth and seventh cords from the right, and tie another Overhand Knot.

6 Pair up the remainder of the cords and tie an Overhand Knot with each pair as in Step 5.

3 Continue to create a series of Spiral Knots until your work measures approximately 18 in. (45 cm) in length. As you tie the knots, your work will start to spiral and create the desired effect. Put the necklace aside.

4 To make the gem case, take the four shorter lengths of cord, fold each in half, and tie an Overhand Knot (see page 11).

7 Continue to pair up the cords in this way until your work resembles a little netted sack and is large enough to hold your gem. Put the gem in the net bag. Then simply pull tight and work a final Overhand Knot with all of the cords. Snip off the excess cord to the desired length.

8 Slip the netted gem and case onto your spiral necklace cord. Finish off the piece by securing the ends of the necklace cords in a fold-over cord end and attaching a jump ring and lobster clasp for fastening the necklace (see Finishing a Project, page 26).

Interesting shapes
The gemstone is really
the star of this piece,
and the shape and
color of the stone will
make a pretty impact
on your necklace.

Chevron Bracelet

This charming little bracelet is quick and easy to make using Left and Right Full Loop Knots.

YOU WILL NEED:

- 2 lengths of embroidery thread, measuring approx. 30 in. (76 cm), in 3 colors
- 2 lengths of crochet thread, measuring approx. 30 in. (76 cm) in gold
- 2 x ribbon clamps
- 2 x 6 mm jump rings
- 1 x lobster clasp
- Needle-nosed pliers

SKILL LEVEL: INTERMEDIATE

Dimensions
- Length: 7 in. (18 cm)
- Width: ½ in. (1.3 cm)

Knot Finder
- Left Full Loop Knot, see page 14
- Right Full Loop Knot, see page 15

Sunny style
The brightly colored cords used here make this cheerful bracelet a great choice for summer!

1 Attach all of the cords to one of the ribbon clamps, arranging the colors as shown here, with the gold crochet threads on the outside.

2 Using the thread on the far left of your work, create a series of Left Full Loop Knots (see page 14) over the next three threads.

3 Using the thread on the far right of your work, create a series of Right Full Loop Knots (see page 15) over the next three threads. Then knot the two new (gold crochet) inner threads together with a Right Full Loop Knot.

4 Repeat Steps 2–3 until your work measures approximately 6½ in. (16.5 cm) in length or the desired length for your wrist. Finish off the piece by placing the ends of the cords in the other ribbon clamp, and attaching jump rings and a lobster clasp for fastening the bracelet (see Finishing a Project, page 26).

Lapis Earrings

These are charming and sophisticated earrings, with a hint of Egyptian inspiration.

YOU WILL NEED:

- 6 lengths of micro-macramé cord, measuring approx. 30 in. (76 cm)
- 2 x 3-hole earring hangers
- 2 x ear wires
- 52 size 11 seed beads in Color A
- 40 size 11 seed beads in Color B
- 2 x 6 mm lapis beads
- 4 x 4 mm lapis beads
- Needle-nosed pliers

SKILL LEVEL: INTERMEDIATE

Dimensions (each)
- Length: 3 1/4 in. (8.5 cm)
- Width: 3/4 in. (2 cm)

Knot Finder
- Lark's Head Knot, see page 10
- Double Half Hitch Knot, see pages 16–17
- Overhand Knot, see page 11

Earring hangers
These useful findings are available in many different designs and finishes. Shop around to find some that suit your style.

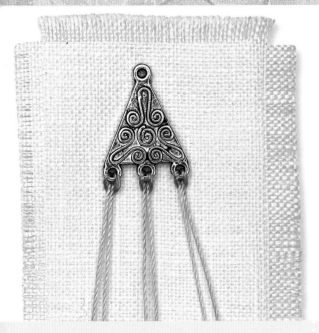

1 Fold three of the cords in half and attach them individually to one of the earring hangers using Lark's Head Knots (see page 10).

2 Starting at the left-hand side of your work, make a row of Double Half Hitch Knots (see pages 16–17), parallel to the earring hanger.

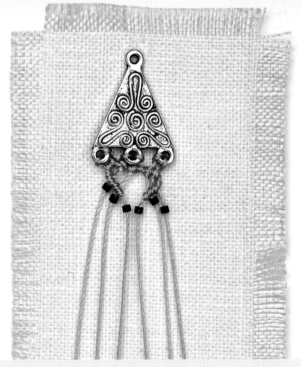

3 Using the first three cords on the left, and starting at the outside, work one row of diagonal Double Half Hitch Knots. Then repeat this process with the first three cords on the right, again starting at the outside.

4 Thread one size 11 seed bead in Color A onto each cord.

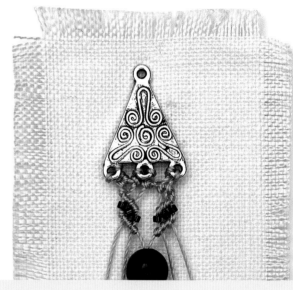

5 Repeat Step 3.

6 Thread the two central cords through one of the 6 mm lapis beads.

7 Thread five size 11 seed beads in Color A onto the outermost cord on the left, followed by one of the 4 mm beads. Add a further five size 11 seed beads in Color A. Thread ten size 11 seed beads in Color B onto the next cord. Then work two rows of Double Half Hitch Knots, starting with the third cord from the left and working right to left.

8 Repeat Step 7 with the cords on the right, reversing the direction of the beads and knots. Then tie one Overhand Knot (see page 11) with all of the cords. Snip off the excess cord, leaving some tassels, and attach an ear wire to the earring hanger, as you would attach a jump ring (see Finishing a Project, page 26). Repeat the process for the second earring.

Multi-Stranded Friendship Bracelet

You can mix and match the colors in this three-in-one bracelet to create your very own fashionable, friendship-style bracelet.

YOU WILL NEED:

- 2 lengths of micro-macramé cord, measuring approx. 50 in. (127 cm), in Color A
- 4 lengths of micro-macramé cord, measuring approx. 50 in. (127 cm), in Color B
- Approx. 30 3–4 mm cube beads
- 1 x focal button with a shank large enough to thread 4 cords through
- 1 x 10 mm split ring
- 1 x ribbon clamp
- 1 x 6 mm jump ring
- 1 x lobster clasp
- Needle-nosed pliers

SKILL LEVEL: INTERMEDIATE

Dimensions
- Length: 7½ in. (19 cm)
- Width: 1 in. (2.5 cm)

Knot Finder
- Lark's Head Knot, see page 10
- Spiral Knot, see page 13
- Square Knot, see page 12

Keep it simple
You could use just one color of micro-macramé cord for a more understated look.

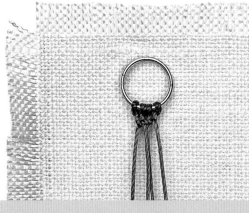

1 Take the two cords in Color A, fold them in half, and attach them individually to the split ring using Lark's Head Knots (see page 10). You now have a total of four cords to work with.

2 Tie a Spiral Knot (see page 13).

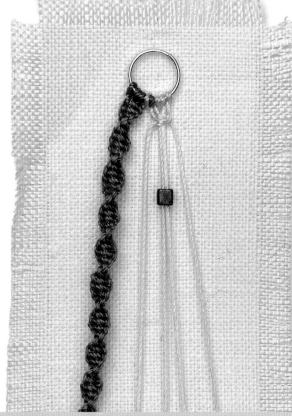

5 Create one Square Knot (see page 12).

6 Thread the two inner cords through one of the 3–4 mm cube beads and push the bead up to the bottom of the Square Knot.

3 Continue to work a series of Spiral Knots until your work measures approximately 7 in. (18 cm) in length or the desired length for your wrist. As you tie the knots, your work will start to spiral and create the desired effect.

4 Repeat Step 1, but this time using two of the Color B cords.

7 Repeat Steps 5 and 6 until your work measures approximately 7 in. (18 cm) in length or the desired length for your wrist.

8 Repeat Steps 1–3 with the remaining two cords in Color B, threading on a focal button half way through your work. Snip off the excess cord on all three strands. Finish the piece by placing the ends of the cords in a ribbon clamp, and attaching a jump ring and lobster clasp for fastening the bracelet (see Finishing a Project, page 26).

Neon Striped Bracelet

This striped creation is the ideal project for practicing the art of the Double Half Hitch Knot. Your practice could very well turn out to be a surprisingly favorite piece.

YOU WILL NEED

- 2 lengths of micro-macramé cord, measuring approx. 40 in. (102 cm), in 3 colors (Colors A, B, and C)
- 4 lengths of micro-macramé cord, measuring approx. 40 in. (102 cm), in Color D
- 2 x ribbon clamps
- 2 x 6 mm jump rings
- 1 x lobster clasp
- Needle-nose pliers

SKILL LEVEL: INTERMEDIATE

Dimensions
- Length: 7 in. (18 cm)
- Width: $\frac{1}{2}$ in. (1.3 cm)

Knot Finder
- Double Half Hitch Knot, see pages 16–17

Bright stripes
These neon colors really pack a punch! Using two neutral colors in the mix would result in a very different look.

1 Attach and enclose all of the cords in one of the ribbon clamps, as shown here. Make sure you place two lengths of Color D on each side.

2 Starting with the cord on the far right, work a row of Double Half Hitch Knots (see pages 16–17) parallel to the ribbon clamp.

3 Starting with the cord on the far left, work another row of Double Half Hitch Knots.

4 Repeat Steps 2–3 until your work measures approximately 6½ in. (16.5 cm) in length or the desired length for your wrist, then snip off the excess cords. Finish by placing the ends of the cords in the second ribbon clamp, and attaching jump rings and a lobster clasp for fastening the bracelet (see Finishing a Project, page 26).

4

Advanced Projects

Now that you've built up a wealth of knotting and beading skills, it's time to show them off with these intricate and impressive jewelry pieces. Concentrate, keep calm, and keep count, and you'll find these projects achievable and rewarding.

Tropical Waves Cuff

This extravagant and striking bracelet demonstrates how choosing large beads can turn little waves into big breakers.

YOU WILL NEED:

- 6 lengths of micro-macramé cord, measuring approx. 60 in. (152.5 cm)
- Approx. 42 size 11 seed beads
- Approx. 250 size 8 seed beads in 2 colors: 160 in Color A and 90 in Color B
- Approx. 50 size 6 seed beads
- 1 x 10 mm split ring
- 1 x ribbon clamp
- 1 x 6 mm jump ring
- 1 x lobster clasp
- Needle-nose pliers

SKILL LEVEL: ADVANCED

Dimensions
- Length: 7 in. (18 cm)
- Width: 1 in. (2.5 cm)

Knot Finder
- Lark's Head Knot, see page 10
- Double Half Hitch Knot, see pages 16–17

1 Fold the six cords in half and attach them individually to the split ring using Lark's Head Knots (see page 10). You now have a total of 12 cords to work with.

2 Starting with the cord on the far right, make two rows of Double Half Hitch Knots (see pages 16–17), working diagonally downward toward the left, as shown.

reating movement
e structured curves of
e beads really do give
e appearance of
cking waves.

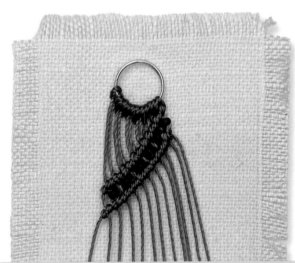

3 Starting with the cord on the far right, thread a size 11 seed bead onto every other cord.

4 Repeat Step 2 to secure the beads.

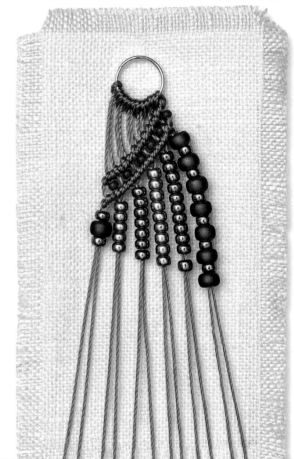

5 Starting from the left, thread the following beads onto the following cords:

- Thread cords 1 and 2 through one size 8 seed bead in Color A, followed by a size 6 seed bead, then another size 8 seed bead in Color A
- Thread cords 3 and 4 through five size 8 seed beads in Color B
- Thread cords 5 and 6 through seven size 8 seed beads in Color A
- Thread cords 7 and 8 through nine size 8 seed beads in Color B
- Thread cords 9 and 10 through 11 size 8 seed beads in Color A
- Thread cords 11 and 12 through one size 6 seed bead, then one size 8 seed bead in Color A. Repeat the sequence until you have seven size 6 and six size 8 seed beads on these two cords.

6 Starting with the cord on the far left, work one row of Double Half Hitch Knots along the bottom edge of this beaded section.

7 Repeat Step 3 to add another row of size 11 seed beads. Repeat Step 6.

8 Starting from the right this time, repeat the threading sequence from Step 5.

9 Starting with the cord on the far right, work one row of Double Half Hitch Knots along the bottom edge of this beaded section.

Rows of Double Half Hitch Knots secure and shape the beaded sections

Size 6, size 8, and size 11 seed beads threaded onto the cords (Step 5)

A 7 in. bracelet will contain approximately six "waves"

10 Repeat Step 3 to add another row of size 11 seed beads.

11 Repeat Step 9 to secure the beads.

12 Repeat Steps 5–11 until your bracelet measures approximately 6½ in. (16.5 cm) in length or the desired length for your wrist.

13 To finish, snip off the excess cords, place the ends of the cords in a ribbon clamp, and attach a jump ring and lobster clasp for fastening the bracelet (see Finishing a Project, page 26).

Stormy Gray Waves Bracelet

This is a subtle and intricate little bracelet made of waves in gray and neutral beads. It shows off the Double Half Hitch Knot at its best.

Showcase your skills
With the intricate pattern of beads and knots, you're sure to impress your friends with this creation.

YOU WILL NEED:

- 5 lengths of micro-macramé cord, measuring approx. 60 in. (152.5 cm)
- Approx. 400 size 11 seed beads in 3 colors: 112 in Color A, 160 in Color B, and 128 in Color C. Here, "Color C" is a mix of several different colors
- 1 x 10 mm split ring
- 1 x ribbon clamp
- 2 x 6 mm jump rings
- 1 x lobster clasp
- Needle-nose pliers

SKILL LEVEL: ADVANCED

Dimensions
- Length: 7 in. (18 cm)
- Width: ¾ in. (2 cm)

Knot Finder
- Lark's Head Knot, see page 10
- Double Half Hitch Knot, see pages 16–17

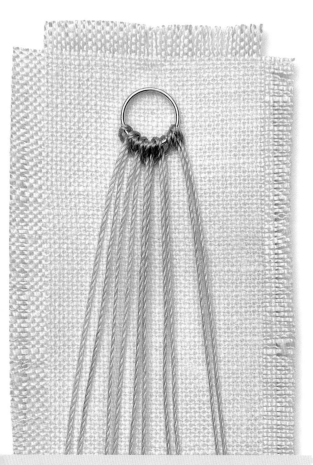

1 Fold the five cords in half and attach them individually to the split ring using Lark's Head Knots (see page 10). You now have a total of ten cords to work with.

2 Starting with the cord on the far right, work two parallel rows of Double Half Hitch Knots (see pages 16–17), working diagonally downward toward the left, as shown.

Five cords folded in half and attached with Lark's Head Knots give 10 working cords (Step 1)

Color C is a mix of several colored beads

Rows of Double Half Hitch Knots secure the beaded sections

The bead quantities listed will create eight "waves"

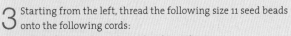

3 Starting from the left, thread the following size 11 seed beads onto the following cords:
  - Thread cord 1 through one bead in Color A
  - Thread cord 2 through two beads in Color A
  - Thread cord 4 through seven beads in Color B
  - Thread cord 6 through 11 beads in Color A
  - Thread cord 8 through 13 beads in Color B
  - Thread cord 10 through 16 beads in Color C

4 Starting with the cord on the far left, work two rows of Double Half Hitch Knots along the bottom edge of this beaded section.

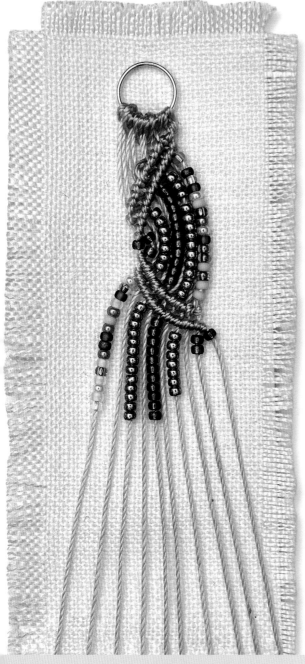

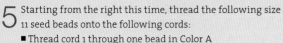

5 Starting from the right this time, thread the following size 11 seed beads onto the following cords:
- Thread cord 1 through one bead in Color A
- Thread cord 2 through two beads in Color A
- Thread cord 4 through seven beads in Color B
- Thread cord 6 through 11 beads in Color A
- Thread cord 8 through 13 beads in Color B
- Thread cord 10 through 16 beads in Color C

6 Starting with the cord on the far right, complete two rows of Double Half Hitch Knots along the bottom edge of this beaded section.

Mix it up
Varying the size of the beads that you use, as shown here, can have a huge impact on the finished piece. Don't be afraid to experiment.

7 Repeat Steps 3–6 to add more "waves."

8 Repeat Steps 3–6 until your work measures approximately 6¹/₂ in. (16.5 cm) in length or the desired length for your wrist. To finish, snip off the excess cords, place the ends in a ribbon clamp, and attach jump rings and a lobster clasp for fastening the bracelet (see Finishing a Project, page 26).

Shimmer and shine
The clear seed beads used in this design shimmer in the light and really add some sparkle to this bracelet.

YOU WILL NEED:

- 2 lengths of micro-macramé cord, measuring approx. 90 in. (228 cm), in 3 colors (Colors A, B, and C)
- Approx. 140 size 8 seed beads
- 1 x focal button with a shank large enough to thread 12 cords through
- 1 x 10 mm split ring
- 1 x ribbon clamp
- 1 x 6 mm jump ring
- 1 x lobster clasp
- Needle-nose pliers

SKILL LEVEL: ADVANCED

Dimensions
- Length: 8½ in. (21.5 cm)
- Width: ¾ in. (2 cm)

Knot Finder
- Lark's Head Knot, see page 10
- Square Knot, see page 12

Beads and Braid Bracelet

This lovely bracelet takes some concentration but is easy to create once you get into a rhythm. The addition of braids makes it even more attractive.

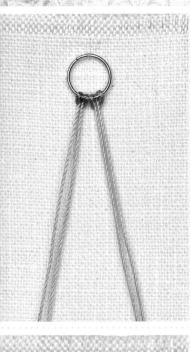

1 Fold the two Color A cords in half and attach them individually to the split ring using Lark's Head Knots (see page 10). You now have a total of four cords to work with.

2 Tie one Square Knot (see page 12).

5 Repeat Steps 1–4 with the cords in Color B and then Color C.

6 Using all three beaded cords, create a simple braid until you reach the end of the cords.

3 Thread the two inner cords through one of the seed beads.

4 Repeat Steps 2 and 3 until your work measures approximately 4 in. (10 cm) in length.

7 Carefully thread all of the cords through the focal button, making sure that the braids are kept neatly in place.

8 Repeat Steps 2–4 for each color cord and then repeat Step 6 to braid together. Finish off the piece by placing the ends of the cords in a ribbon clamp, and attaching a jump ring and lobster clasp for fastening the bracelet (see Finishing a Project, page 26).

Lacy Earrings

So delicate and so pretty, these earrings really do look and feel like lace.

YOU WILL NEED:

- 8 lengths of micro-macramé cord, measuring approx. 25 in. (63.5 cm)
- 2 x 6 mm beads
- 20 size 11 seed beads in Color A
- 48 size 11 seed beads in Color B
- 12 size 8 seed beads
- 4 x 10 mm split ring
- 2 x 6 mm bead charms
- 2 x 6 mm jump rings
- 2 x ear wires
- Needle-nose pliers
- Craft glue

SKILL LEVEL: ADVANCED

Dimensions (each)
- Length: 2½ in. (6.5 cm)
- Width: ¾ in. (2 cm)

Knot Finder
- Lark's Head Knot, see page 10
- Double Half Hitch Knot, see pages 16–17

Soft and subtle
The subtle variations of blue combined with the white add to the dainty look and feel of these earrings.

1 Fold four cords in half and attach them individually to one of the split rings using Lark's Head Knots (page 10). You now have a total of eight cords to work with.

2 Divide the cords into two groups and work each set of four cords separately. Starting with the cord on the far left-hand side, work two rows of Double Half Hitch Knots (see pages 16–17). Repeat the process with the right-hand set of cords, starting with the cord on the far right-hand side.

3 Thread the two central cords (one from each set of four) through one of the 6 mm beads.

4 Thread five size 11 seed beads in Color A onto the third cord from the left.

5 Using the fourth cord from the left, tie one Double Half Hitch Knot over the next cord to its left.

6 Thread one size 8 seed bead onto the second cord from the left.

9 Repeat Steps 6–8 twice more.

10 Using the second cord from the left, tie a Double Half Hitch Knot over the third cord from the left, then over the fourth cord from the left.

7 Thread four size 11 seed beads in Color B onto the outermost cord on the left.

8 Using the far left-hand cord, tie one Double Half Hitch Knot over the next cord to its right.

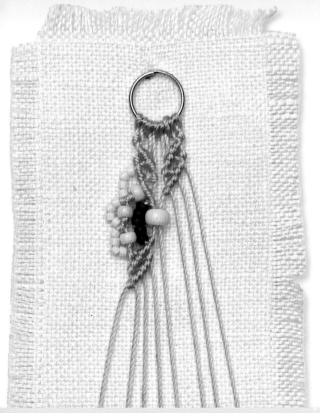

11 Using the left-hand four cords, make a row of Double Half Hitch Knots working from right to left.

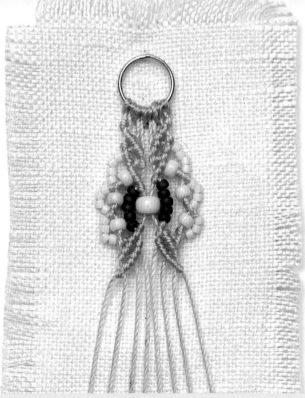

12 Repeat the pattern of Steps 4–11 using the right-hand set of four cords.

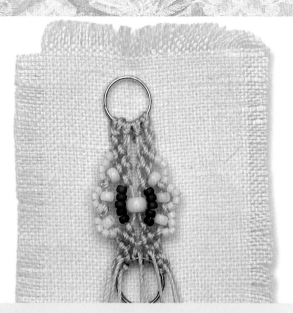

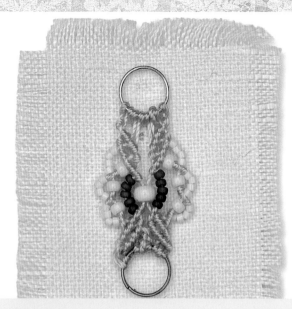

13 Attach all of the cords to a split ring using Lark's Heads Knots. You will find this is easier to do if you turn your work upside down.

14 Pull the knots really tight, then snip off the ends, close to the knot. Dab a little craft glue onto the knots to stop them from coming undone.

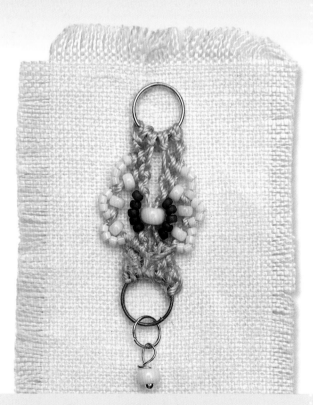

15 Use a jump ring to connect the bead charm to the bottom split ring (see Finishing a Project, page 26).

16 Attach the ear wire to the top split ring, as you would attach a jump ring (see Finishing a Project, page 26). Repeat Steps 1–16 to complete the matching pair.

Owl Bracelet

This bracelet has an unusual design and the pattern of leaf-like shapes is yet another way of using the Double Half Hitch Knot.

YOU WILL NEED:

- 12 lengths of micro-macramé cord, measuring approx. 45 in. (114.5 cm)
- Approx. 200 size 11 seed beads in various colors
- 4 size 8 seed beads
- 1 x focal connector charm with 2 holes at each end
- 2 x ribbon clamps
- 2 x 6 mm jump rings
- 1 x lobster clasp
- Needle-nose pliers

SKILL LEVEL: ADVANCED

Dimensions
- Length: 7 in. (18 cm)
- Width: 1 in. (2.5 cm)

Knot Finder
- Lark's Head Knot, see page 10
- Double Half Hitch Knot, see pages 16–17

Change the focus
If you use a smaller focal connector, add another repeat of beads and knots on each side.

1 Fold six of the cords in half and attach them individually to the focal connector using Lark's Head Knots (see page 10). You now have a total of 12 cords to work with.

2 Work two rows of Double Half Hitch Knots (see pages 16–17). Start the first row with the cord on the far left, and then start the second row with the cord on the far right.

5 Divide the cords into two groups and work each set of six cords separately. Work with the left-hand set of cords first. Starting with the sixth cord from the left, create one row of Double Half Hitch Knots across all the other cords on the left, working diagonally downward, as shown.

6 Work another row of Double Half Hitch Knots as in Step 5, but omit the last cord on the left.

3 Starting with the cord on the far right, thread one size 11 seed bead onto every other cord.

4 Repeat Step 2.

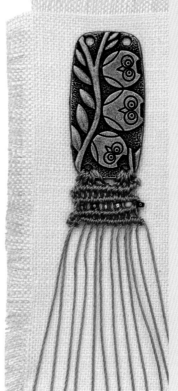

7 Work another row of Double Half Hitch Knots, but omit the last two cords on the left.

8 Work another row of Double Half Hitch Knots, but omit the last three cords on the left.

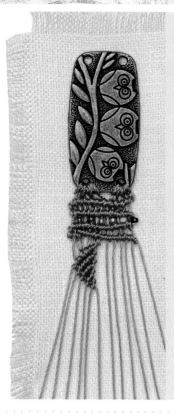

9 Tie one final Double Half Hitch Knot with the two innermost cords in the left-hand group.

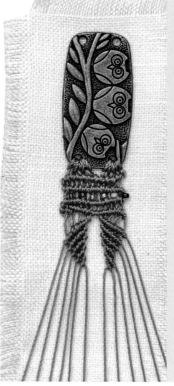

10 Repeat Steps 5–9 with the cords on the right of your work, starting with the sixth cord from the right and working diagonally downward from right to left.

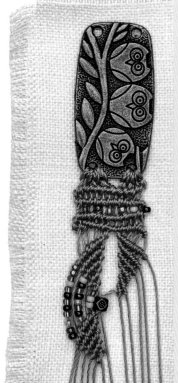

13 Repeat Steps 5–9.

14 Repeat Step 12 with the cords on the right of your work, starting from the far right cord. Then repeat Step 10.

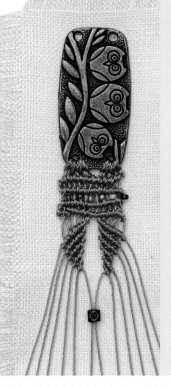

11 Thread the two central cords (one from each set of six) through one of the size 8 seed beads.

12 Starting from the far left cord, thread the following size 11 seed beads onto the following cords:
- Thread cord 1 through 12 beads
- Thread cord 3 through 8 beads
- Thread cord 5 through 3 beads

15 Repeat Steps 11–14 once more, then snip off the excess cords. Place the ends of the cords in a ribbon clamp, and attach a jump ring (see Finishing a Project, page 26).

Repeat Steps 1–15 again, attaching the cords in Step 1 to the other side of the focal connector. Attach a lobster clasp for fastening the bracelet to one of the jump rings to finish.

Rows of Double Half Hitch Knots (Steps 2–4)

Attach the cords to the focal connector to begin each side of the bracelet

Double Half Hitch Knots worked on the diagonal create leaf-like patterns

Baroque Bracelet

This is a sophisticated bracelet with oodles of charm and high-class appeal.

YOU WILL NEED:

- 4 lengths of micro-macramé cord, measuring approx. 60 in. (152.5 cm)
- Approx. 6 x 6 mm focal beads
- Approx. 5 x 8 mm focal beads
- Approx. 200 size 11 seed beads
- Approx. 30 size 8 seed beads
- 1 x 10 mm split ring
- 1 x ribbon clamp
- 2 x 6 mm jump rings
- 1 x lobster clasp
- Needle-nosed pliers

SKILL LEVEL: ADVANCED

Dimensions
- Length: 7 in. (18 cm)
- Width: ¾ in. (2 cm)

Knot Finder
- Lark's Head Knot, see page 10
- Double Half Hitch Knot, see pages 16–17

1 Fold the four cords in half and attach them individually to the split ring using Lark's Head Knots (see page 10). You now have a total of eight cords to work with.

2 Divide the cords into two groups and work each set of four cords separately. Starting with the fourth cord from the left, work two rows of Double Half Hitch Knots (see pages 16–17), working diagonally downward toward the left, as shown. Repeat with the cords on the right, starting with the fourth cord from the right and working diagonally downward toward the right.

ersonalize it

different style or color of
cal bead could make
s a totally new bracelet.

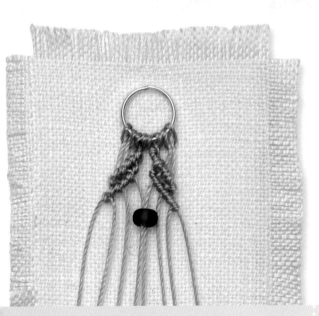

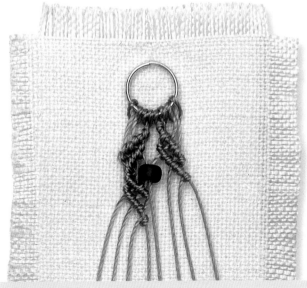

3 Thread the two central cords (one from each set of four) through one of the 6 mm focal beads.

4 Starting with the cord on the far left, work two rows of Double Half Hitch Knots over the following three cords to the right.

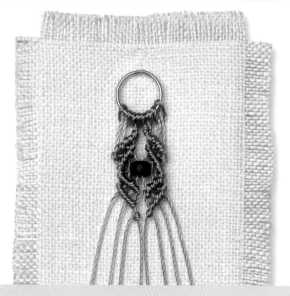

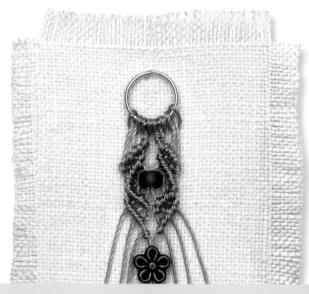

5 Repeat Step 4 using the right-hand cords, starting with the cord on the far right and working from right to left.

6 Thread the two central cords (one from each set of four) through one of the 8 mm focal beads.

8 Using the third cord from the left, tie a Double Half Hitch Knot over the next cord to the right to secure the beads.

9 Thread one of the size 8 seed beads onto the second cord from the left.

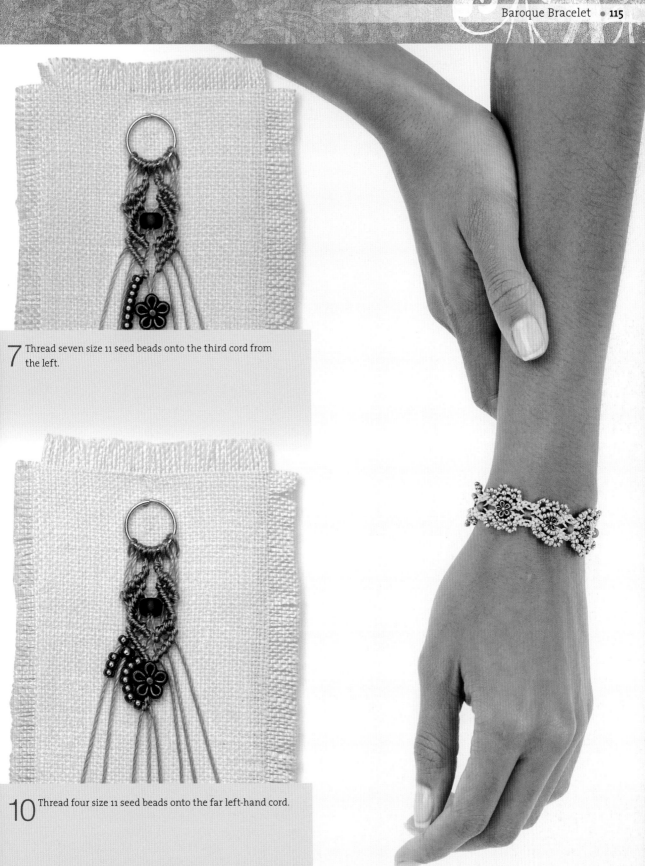

7 Thread seven size 11 seed beads onto the third cord from the left.

10 Thread four size 11 seed beads onto the far left-hand cord.

11 Using the outermost cord on the left, work one Double Half Hitch Knot over the next cord to its right.

12 Repeat Steps 9–11 twice more.

15 Repeat the pattern of Steps 7–14 using the cords on the right-hand side of your work.

16 Repeat Steps 3–15 until your work measures approximately 6½ in. (16.5 cm) in length or the desired length for your wrist. To finish, snip off the excess cords, place the ends in a ribbon clamp, and attach jump rings and a lobster clasp for fastening the bracelet (see Finishing a Project, page 26).

13 Starting with the third cord from the left, and working from right to left, work a row of Double Half Hitch Knots.

14 Starting with the fourth cord from the left, and working from right to left, work a row of Double Half Hitch Knots.

Double Half Hitch Knots separate the sections of beading

6 mm focal bead threaded onto the two central cords (Step 3)

Cords secured to the split ring with Lark's Head Knots (Step 1)

Focal bead surrounded by size 8 and size 11 seed beads

The bead quantities given will create five beaded sections

Tassel Necklace

This fun and funky necklace has a tribal look to it. You can choose the length of the tassels to make it as big and bold as you wish.

YOU WILL NEED:

- 10 lengths of waxed cord, measuring 0.6 mm in diameter and approx. 30 in. (76 cm) in length
- 1 length of waxed cord, measuring 0.6 mm in diameter and approx. 20 in. (51 cm) in length
- 10 size 8 seed beads
- 2 x fold-over cord ends
- 2 x 6 mm jump rings
- 1 x lobster clasp
- Needle-nose pliers

SKILL LEVEL: ADVANCED

Dimensions
- Length: 20 in. (51 cm)
- Width: As desired

Knot Finder
- Larks Head Knot, see page 10
- Double Half Hitch Knot, see pages 16–17

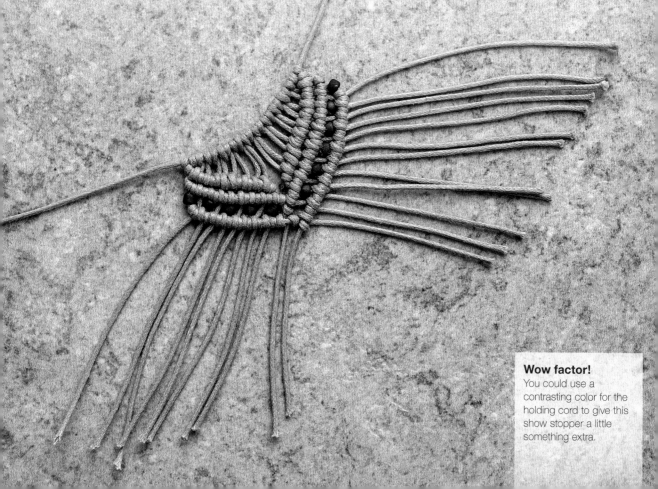

Wow factor!
You could use a contrasting color for the holding cord to give this show stopper a little something extra.

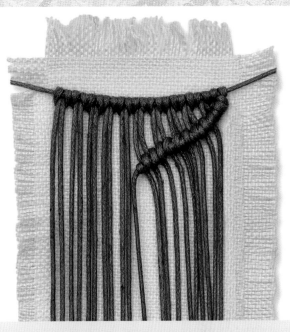

1 Fold the 10 long cords in half and attach them individually to the center of the 20 in. holding cord using Lark's Head Knots (see page 10). You now have a total of 20 cords to work with.

2 Divide the cords into two groups of 10. Starting with the far right-hand cord and working over the right-hand set of 10 cords, work one row of Double Half Hitch Knots (see pages 16–17). Work diagonally downward toward the left, as shown.

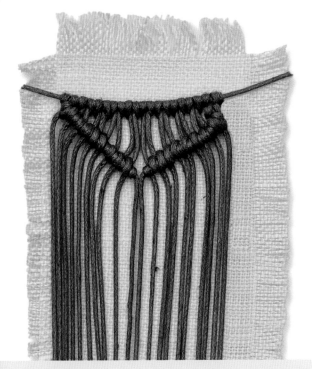

3 Starting with the far left-hand cord and working over the left-hand set of 10 cords, work one row of Double Half Hitch Knots. Work diagonally downward toward the right, as shown.

4 Repeat Steps 2–3.

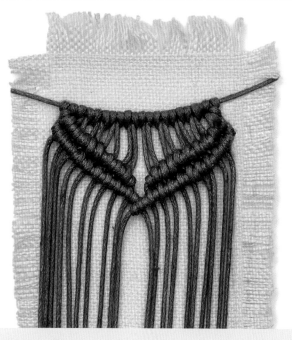

5 Tie the two central cords (one from each set of 10) together using a Double Half Hitch Knot.

6 Starting with one of the outermost cords, thread a size 8 seed bead onto every other cord but leave out the two central cords. Use this picture as a guide.

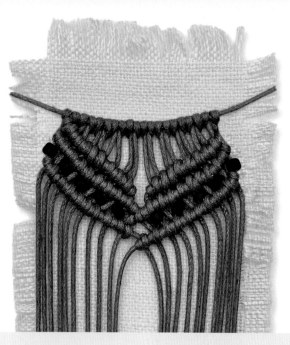

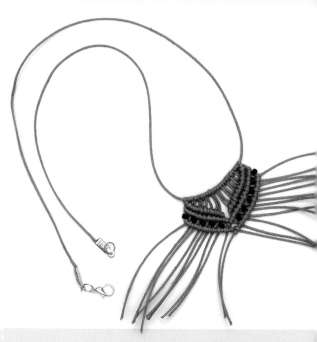

7 Repeat Steps 2 and 3 once more, then repeat Step 5.

8 To finish, trim the cords to the desired length for the necklace, attach a fold-over cord end and jump ring to both ends of the necklace, and then attach a lobster clasp for fastening (see Finishing a Project, page 26).

Lace Choker

This very delicate and pretty choker may take you a little longer to make, but the end result will definitely be worth it.

YOU WILL NEED:

- 6 lengths of micro-macramé cord, measuring approx. 60 in. (152.5 cm), in color of choice
- Approx. 84 size 11 seed beads
- 1 x 10 mm split ring
- 1 x ribbon clamp
- 1 x 6 mm jump ring
- 1 x lobster clasp
- Needle-nose pliers

SKILL LEVEL: ADVANCED

Dimensions
- Length: 14½ in. (37 cm)
- Width: ½ in. (1.3 cm)

Knot Finder
- Larks Head Knot, see page 10
- Square Knot, see page 12

Clean and classic
Keeping the beading just to the edge of this intricate piece stops it from looking too busy.

1 Fold the six cords in half and attach them individually to the split ring using Lark's Head Knots (see page 10). You now have a total of 12 cords to work with.

2 Divide the cords into three groups of four and work each set of cords separately.

5 Tie the right-hand set of four cords together using a Square Knot.

6 Starting with the third cord from the left, tie the next four cords to the right together using a Square Knot. The two cords on the far left should remain loose, as shown.

3 Using the left-hand set of four cords, tie together using a Square Knot (see page 12).

4 Tie the central set of four cords together using a Square Knot.

7 Starting with the seventh cord from the left, tie the next four cords to the right together using a Square Knot. The two cords on the far right should remain loose, as shown.

8 Thread one size 11 seed bead onto the far left-hand cord.

9 Repeat Step 3.

10 Repeat Step 4.

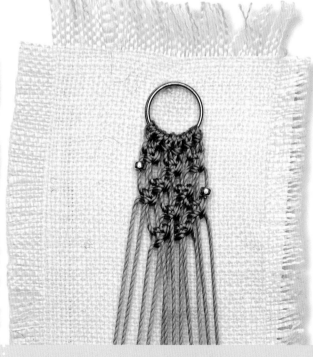

11 Thread one size 11 seed bead onto the far right-hand cord. Then, repeat Step 5.

12 Repeat Steps 6–11 until your work measures approximately 14 in. (35.5 cm) in length, or your desired length, then trim the excess cords. Finish by placing the ends of the cords in a ribbon clamp, and attaching a jump ring and lobster clasp for fastening the choker (see Finishing a Project, page 26).

Index

Credits

Author acknowledgments

I'd like to say thank you to Spoilt Rotten Beads for their huge selection of cords and beads.
   Also, a big thank you to my husband for all his support, and an extra big thank you to my 20-year-old cat and 20-year-old ex-racehorse for just being there at the end of each day!
   Last but not least, thanks to Lily de Gatacre for making working on this book simply a pleasure.

Many thanks to Spoilt Rotten Beads for kindly supplying materials for the creation of the projects in this book.

Spoilt Rotten
BEADS

7 The Green, Haddenham,
Ely, Cambridgeshire,
CB6 3TA
01353 749853
www.spoiltrottenbeads.co.uk